SPIRITUAL CHANGEMAKERS

TOWARDS A BETTER WORLD

ISOBEL BLACKTHORN

CONTENTS

INTRODUCING THE ESOTERIC
ROOTS OF TWELVES

" Twelves is definitely an esoteric adventure and
we are pioneers.

— PATRICK CHOUINARD

For some time I have wanted to write another non-fiction
book that draws on the particular form of esoteric knowledge I know most about, Theosophy, focusing on the
particular version of Theosophy advanced by Alice A.
Bailey and the tradition her work set. Many times I have
been asked to write an introductory guide to the Bailey
teachings. I did consider it, but I didn't want to go down
the path of summary and explanation. Not when
humanity faces a monumental crisis of its own making, or
rather multiple crises that have brought our very existence
to the brink of extinction.

In my view, at this critical juncture in history, esoteric
knowledge and knowing must answer to the current
global situation. Somehow, esoteric knowledge must grant
us the power to re-imagine our future. If not, there is
nothing of vital spiritual value in the worldview. After all,

science has made itself utterly relevant to the times. Scientists heed and answer the call to preserve and protect humanity and the planet at every turn. Religion, the way of faith, offers solace and comfort and healing, and it, too, heeds the historical moment.

What is the esoteric community doing, if anything, to help the world?

The Bailey books were written as progressive and forward-thinking. They offer the possibility of advanced esoteric training which can be gained through Alice Bailey's Arcane School, The School for Esoteric Studies, and other organisations. Much can be achieved by simply studying the books themselves. Here can be found a special kind of psychological training. This training of the mind – spiritual in essence – can benefit the individual, but its fruits are meant to go far beyond the self. If not, as Alice Bailey stresses many times in her books, esoteric knowledge and practice soon descend into the path of darkness. Esoteric knowledge for its own sake, or for the aggrandisement of the individual, is anathema to all Alice Bailey stood for.

Realising this, I became interested in portraying the foundations being laid today by those inspired by the Ageless Wisdom offered in the Bailey books to help shape a bright and healthy future. A future in which groups of individuals work together in illuminated ways.

Most of us approach esoteric knowledge and practice with a mind filled with fascination. Some may carry a desire for power or personal gain. There's a definite mystique when it comes to hidden or secret knowledge accessible only to a chosen few, those with a particular and perhaps peculiar disposition, those with an inner eye that can penetrate beyond the veils of ordinary existence.

Many seekers in the esoteric realm start out as mystics. In *Mysticism: A study in the nature and development of Man's spiritual consciousness*, Evelyn Underhill explores mysticism as an 'essential religious experience'.[1] Mysticism is a form of apprehension involving visionary phenomena, tuning in to the reality of an unseen world. For Underhill, the mystic way involves an awakening of the self, followed by the purification and the illumination of the self. Voices and visions, ecstasy and rapture, and contemplation all form part of the life of the mystic. In *Varieties of Religious Experience*, William James writes of mystical states of consciousness as adding 'a supersensuous meaning to the ordinary outward data of consciousness', offering perhaps 'the truest of insights into the meaning of this life'.[2]

The esoteric way differs markedly from its mystic sister. Esotericists claim a higher or metaphysical knowledge and wisdom that has universal explanatory power. Traditionally, and in the West, esotericism – which includes Hermeticism, Gnosticism, Alchemy, Rosicrucianism, Freemasonry, and Theosophy – adheres to a particular cluster of beliefs and practices: secrecy; transmission of knowledge from master to disciple; initiation and revelation; a fundamental unifying principle governing existence; living nature (hylozoism); the idea of correspondence between a macrocosmic universe and a microcosmic human; the ability to mediate between the macro and micro through the use of symbols, images, rituals and intermediary spirits; a belief in transformation; and the existence of the soul.

These briefly described mystic and esoteric ways are distinct yet they share something fundamental: that there exists another world beyond that known through the five senses, beyond reason and beyond science, and that this otherworld can be accessed and known. From this basic outline it's easy to see how the mystic way may attract those of a devotional and emotional nature, and those with rich imaginations, the esoteric way attracting those of a more intellectual bent. That said, the two ways are not mutually exclusive, particularly in the twenty-first century where variations of an amalgamation of these two ways of knowing can be seen in various spiritual modalities.

Another keynote of esoteric practice is the harnessing and directing of energy. While the mystic passively observes or actively experiences metaphysical reality, the esotericist engages in practices of active conscious involvement with it. Here, the intention of the esoteric practitioner is paramount, the practitioner also drawing on the imaginative and illuminated mind of the mystic. The aim of this book is to explore this practice of harnessing and directing energy in group formation for human and planetary betterment. The people involved are spiritual changemakers.

How do the Bailey teachings have anything to say about the saving the planet? In what ways do the teachings inspire followers to act for change?

Alice A Bailey (1880-1949) was born Alice Ann La Trobe-Bateman, a British aristocrat who adopted in her childhood a fervent Christian outlook. It wasn't until she was in her mid-thirties that her traditional faith gave way to a theosophical outlook. By then she was living south of San Francisco in Pacific Grove. Her fervent nature saw her adopting this new philosophy with zeal and she was soon holding classes. She then moved south to Hollywood, Los Angeles, where she joined the community at the Theosophical Society headquarters at Krotona. It was here that she had a vision – a mystical experience – in which she was invited to scribe for a spiritual master.

Alice Bailey was hardly unique. Channelling, or receiving transmissions, or being in telepathic rapport with a higher being, was something of a grail amongst freethinking spiritual seekers of that period. What sets her apart is the quality of the ideas and impressions she received, and their all-encompassing scope.

After finding herself ousted from Krotona, Bailey gathered a team around her and founded a number of organisations to further the work. She continued for thirty years hoping to provide the esoteric foundations for the upcoming new age of Aquarius.

To some extent, the Bailey teachings carry forward her own Christian faith, and with texts as *From Bethlehem to Calvary* and *The Reappearance of The Christ* it is little wonder. Yet to argue that Christian thought underpins Bailey's output would be a gross over-simplification. Central to the texts is the notion of a planetary hierarchy overseeing the evolution of humanity, and one of the departmental heads of this hierarchy is the World Teacher (The Bodhisattva, Maitreya or The Christ). The planetary hierarchy itself is said to operate under the impression of the solar hierarchy along specific energetic pathways of light or energy rays.

These hierarchies in Bailey's scheme are an example of intermediaries central to esoteric thought. Intermediaries as Masters can be found in Jewish mysticism and Renaissance Rosicrucian and Masonic thought.[3] Although it was founder of the Theosophical Society Helena Petrovna Blavatsky who brought the Masters to the foreground of esoteric thinking.

For students and seekers, it doesn't matter if the planetary hierarchy is taken as real, or if the individual acts *as if* the masters are real. What matters is an acceptance of the idea of spiritual intermediaries itself, whether they be angels, avatars, initiates, adepts, guides, gods and goddesses, or masters. These intermediaries populate metaphysical reality, or the inner planes of existence, and are fundamental to mystic and esoteric ways of knowing.

Bailey's view of the spiritual hierarchy carries an Adventist flavour, some of her writing anticipating a second coming of Christ. Alice Bailey wrote during the interwar period and on through World War Two and its aftermath, and the idea of salvation and the need for some form of intervention was paramount. Every good-hearted thinking person of the time knew it. Humanity was then on a precipice. A new and enlightened age must be encouraged. Destruction and devastation through inequality and war must be arrested. Bailey was responding to the moment. Yet the teachings also advance the idea that the spiritual hierarchy meets every hundred years in a conclave. The last meeting took place in 1925, and the next meeting is due sometime around 2025. This upcoming meeting, the teachings stress, will determine the fate of humanity.

> Thus a great and new movement is proceeding and a tremendously increased interplay and interaction is taking place. This will go on until A.D. 2025. During the years intervening between now and then very great changes will be seen taking place, and at the great General Assembly of the Hierarchy—held as usual every century—in 2025 the date in all probability will be set for the first stage of the externalisation of the Hierarchy.
>
> — *THE EXTERNALISATION OF THE HIERARCHY,*
> P. 530

Whether or not this particular view of the spiritual hierarchy is accepted, I think the Bailey teachings provide a valuable way of viewing the world that predisposes us to look after or indeed save it. Pivotal to Bailey is the idea of being of service to humanity. She is concerned with what motivates us and attempts to shift our motivations towards selflessness and a willingness to serve. A core focus of the teachings is working in groups, even as much of the spiritual training concerns the individual. The spiritual path is about de-centralising the personality and becoming soul-centred and in this way growing spiritually. The teachings then tell us to tap into intuitive ways of knowing and function in group formation.

The Bailey teachings were written to be applied. There are numerous examples of Bailey students applying the teachings in esoteric psychology and astrology, in a range of healing modalities, in working to bring about goodwill and peace, in meditation, and in education. Out of this array of activities, I have chosen to explore one example of group work inspired by the Bailey books: Twelves. I chose Twelves because it exemplifies what Alice Bailey most wanted to advance, the ability of individuals to engage in energy work in groups in order to bring about real and positive global change, and to form an active bridge between the hierarchy and humanity. The work is subtle, esoteric, and amounts to pure white magic.

Twelves founder Steven Chernikeeff seeks 'to build a group-work foundation for future workers to expand on'. This book has been written with that in mind, to help Twelves be knowable and discoverable.

Vera Stanley Alder helped raise awareness of the Bailey teachings, presenting them to a wider audience through her books on meditation, the Divine Plan, progressive movements and humanitarianism, and colour therapy and breath work. There was a need and she filled it. I'm always questioning what my role as an author might be regarding Alice Bailey, her books, and this wider community of intermediary beings trying to help humanity. I've made the teachings more accessible by putting them into their historical context, and through applying them to myself in a most humble way and documenting that in my doctoral thesis, I helped open an academic window on esotericism as lived experience. This time, my role is to clothe Twelves in language to help foster a broader understanding of its function and why it is pivotally important. I've adopted an experiential narrative style in the vein of memoir. Rather than write about Twelves, I have strived to show the process of Twelves as I have come to understand it, both from within as a participant. Some chapters are entirely devoted to the philosophy and the rituals of Twelves. Included in the following chapters, along with my own voice, are the voices of others, their backgrounds, their experiences of Twelves and why they joined. Through this diverse multiplicity of voices from all around the world, Spiritual Changemakers is a snapshot of esoteric service.

---

1. Evelyn Underhill, *Mysticism: A study in the nature and development of Man's spiritual consciousness* (New York: Meridian Books, 1955), p vii.
2. William James, The Varieties of Religious Experience (New York: Penguin, 1982), p 428.
3. John Selby, Dion Fortune and her Inner Plane Contacts: Intermediaries in the Western Esoteric Tradition (University of Exeter, PhD thesis), p273.

MY JOURNEY TO TWELVES

I'm offering the following potted autobiography to illustrate how I came to know Twelves. I hope to give some insight into the curious life of a reluctant esotericist who has from time to time felt commandeered to undertake tasks not of her conscious choosing, a woman who looks through the mists at the road ahead with some anticipation.

I came into this world an ordinary if sensitive child of humble parentage. My father's mother was psychic – she read tea leaves and saw ghosts – and my maternal great-grandmother was a devout Spiritualist and faith healer. I was born on her birthday, 19 January. I was also born on the birthday of a distant ancestor on my maternal grandfather's side, Hannah Batts, who was a herbalist healer. There's a Catholic Nun somewhere among my distant aunts, too, who did good work in Ethiopia. There are also a fair few drunken and violent and otherwise unsavoury men sprinkled through my ancestry.

I wasn't cut out to withstand my own father's violent nature. By the time I left home, I carried inside me a wound the size of a mountain and an attitude to go with it.

People thought I was strange. I had dark moods. I was prone to zoning out or going numb. I was reckless. Once or twice in my teenage years I lost control in a fit of hysteria. Strong emotions of separation and unbelonging would swamp me sometimes, and it was as though I had temporarily become someone else. I didn't know this other person within and she didn't know me. In some makeshift fashion, I held my fragmented self together through my twenties while I set about gaining first-class honours at the Open University, UK, while dabbling in Bohemian living and becoming an anti-nuclear activist.

I had my first spiritual moment when I was twenty-four, during a therapeutic energy work session with a man people described as a Yogi. During the session, I filled with euphoria. It was entirely unexpected and absolutely breath-taking and I was walking on air for hours afterwards and felt, rather naively, reborn, as though my troubled past was behind me and from then on, I would live happily ever after.

It was not to be.

But the spiritual journey had definitely opened up to me. I was introduced to the ideas and talks of Krishnamurti about six months later – not that I made much sense of them – and I was re-birthed a few times, thanks to a friend. A few years later, I discovered astrology, and found I had a natural talent for it.

I also learned Reiki and reflexology, did a short course in Jungian psychotherapy and consulted a transpersonal therapist to deal with the multiple selves of my inner landscape. I went on to study for a diploma in transpersonal counselling. The nine-month course was hands-on experiential in style, along the lines of healer heal thyself, and proved highly beneficial. It was there that I met a man who gifted me his second-hand and somewhat battered copy of Alice Bailey's *Esoteric Astrology*. He explained he had no idea why he bought the book, let alone packed it, along with whatever else he could fit in his car, when he left his life back in Adelaide and travelled halfway across Australia to start over. A cynic would say he gifted it to me because he wanted to make room on his bookshelf or he was sick of the sight of that plain blue cover, but when he said the book was meant for me, he was sincere. And as I took the book from his upturned palms, I believed him.

I devoured that book. I'm not sure I understood it that well – it is a very difficult book to truly grasp – but it took me into an esoteric world I had no prior knowledge of. Or so I thought at first, but it soon became apparent that wasn't true. Sometimes I found myself seeing the next page of text before I read it.

I knew that my search for meaning had ended. I would no longer explore alternative modalities. I had, in fact, found a source. I went on to buy the other Bailey books, reading each one indiscriminately and with an unquenchable thirst. I became, momentarily, a snob, looking down on my friends from this new height, privy to secret knowledge that somehow made me special. I recall to this day the way I distanced myself from my then friends. How I drifted away. I started a little Esoteric Astrology class (I was already teaching astrology). I joined the Arcane School and did the meditations. It was all part of a different sort of inner life growing in me, a way of knowing and also a path of self-improvement. With Bailey there was no allowance made for self-indulgence, self-pity or any form of wallowing. You picked yourself up by the bootstraps. You are told to make a contribution. I took all that on and I am sure it helped make me stronger.

I was a very long way from contributing anything to society at that time. I was by then the mother of twin girls, and two years after Bailey entered my life, I entered a very dark period which lasted for many years. I left the Arcane

School. My collection of Bailey books gathered dust on my bookshelf. In this period, the portion of the teachings that resonated with me concerned the tests faced along the spiritual path. The testing was so fierce there were times when I didn't feel equipped to cope, but I got through it all.

By the end of my thirties, thanks to the gruelling nature of life itself, I was an entirely different person. I carried the battle scars. I had the appearance of a startled rabbit. And I was a high school teacher of history and religious studies in the UK.

It was in those religious studies classes that Alice Bailey crept back into my life. I slipped the concept of initiation found in *From Bethlehem to Calvary* into my Year Seven 'Life of Jesus' classes. The teachings filtered into my Year Nine Buddhism classes, too. My meditation class was highly popular. Word went around the school and students would beg me to hold meditations. Bubbling away behind all my lesson plans was a Bailey-inspired worldview along with the associated ethics and sense of purpose. Keen to do something to make a difference, I founded a school link with a school in Ghana, West Africa, which quickly became an exemplar for other schools to follow.

Throughout those few years of teaching, something in me demanded expression. I had both creative and intellectual aspirations. I wanted the satisfaction that comes with completing a PhD, the stimulation of tertiary studies, and the glory of an academic posting. A raft of other circumstances conspired, causing me to leave the teaching profession.

As ever, my academic 'castle in the air' did not shape up to be what I thought it might. I hadn't set out to undertake a doctorate focusing on the Bailey books. The idea was a passing mention in one of my emails to a potential supervisor. She pounced on the idea of researching Alice Bailey, phoned to urge me to study full-time. Before I could catch my breath, my life had turned itself upside-down and I was back living in Australia studying in the School of Social Ecology at Western Sydney University, and I found myself once more in the milieu of transpersonal psychology, along with ideas from ecology and complexity theory and permaculture and all kinds of avant-garde thinking.

Those were heady years. I read most of the Bailey books again and as I did, I kept a journal of my own thoughts and feelings. I read *A Treatise on Cosmic Fire*, *Esoteric Psychology* Volumes I and II, *The Externalisation of the Hierarchy*, the *Discipleship in the New Age* volumes, *Glamour: A World Problem* and many more. I accepted the existence of the spiritual hierarchy, and embraced the concept of the rays and the initiations. I saw and interpreted my own life through the esoteric lens Bailey offered. I wore the books like a second skin.

Studying the Bailey books full-time stretched my intellectual powers to the full. My higher mind was taut, sharp, cutting. For a couple of years, I succumbed to that seductive veil of intellectual pride. I felt superior even as I fought against it. I had a grand vision, one that would develop the most far-reaching of Bailey's ideas along the lines of inclusivity and holistic awareness and interconnectedness. I then came up hard against a paradox. How can you be inclusive and then exclude all thinking, all ideas that are not inclusive in the way you want them to be? The entire vision I had built in my mind grew to be absurd. My heart was clearly not that involved or I would never have fallen foul of this elitism. I was in danger of becoming wooden and pompous, although the larger part of me was never going to let that happen. Besides, there never was an academic posting in the offing and my castle in the air popped.

I went from receiving my PhD to the very next year working as personal assistant to a literary agent who represented all manner of professors from prestigious universities, including a Nobel prize winner, along with the cream of Australian journalists, politicians and social commentators. I felt pea-sized. I had to swallow my lowly status and do my job. To add to my frustrations, my boss urged me to write a biography of Alice Bailey, but I had no idea how to go about it. There was very little history in my doctorate, which was grounded in phenomenology and profoundly experiential. And besides, Bailey's key organisation the Lucis Trust were in my experience a closed book.

In the year I worked for the literary agency, I developed a friendship with an author who offered to mentor me in creative writing. It was an extraordinary gift which I accepted with much delight. I was finally able to realise my lifelong dream to write fiction. I was forty-seven years old. My daughters were turning eighteen and it was my time now.

I worked very hard at creative writing. Writing filled me with joy. Honouring my creative self, my muse, was singly the most powerful healing move I could possibly have undertaken. The pen is a gift and I treasure it and respect it and serve its will.

Alice Bailey was far, far away from me during this time and yet also awfully close. I say Alice Bailey even as I know that those in the milieu speak of the Master DK (the Tibetan or Djwhal Khul) who is considered to have influenced the writing of most of the Bailey books through a process of impression or telepathic rapport. I am not going to dispute that. But it is with Alice Bailey herself that I feel a real closeness. It is her voice that guides me, as much by her example, and through the rapport I have with her, a sense of something shared.

In late 2016, with three novels published, I contacted my former boss at the literary agency seeking her advice about a novel I was planning. I attached a synopsis. I am not sure she read it. She replied the next day with a single line saying she simply didn't know why I wouldn't write a biography of Alice Bailey. Something in me clicked. By then I felt I had acquired enough creative writing skills to pull it off, although I was hesitant walking back into non-fiction.

The next few months I worked furiously hard. I produced a draft biography and a book proposal. I submitted both to publishers and agents but no one took any interest. I shelved the project. Then in late-2017, I had the idea to transform the biography into a novel. By the following April I had a first draft and in December 2018, *The Unlikely Occultist* was published.

In the year it took to turn my draft biography into a fictional narrative, it was as though I was sitting on a rug at Alice's knee. I moved in to almost every house she lived in. I journeyed with her through all of her life's difficulties. I did my best to think as she did, feel as she did in a process akin to indwelling. My respect and love for Alice grew and grew. I felt I was her arch supporter, advocate, ambassador and defender. What of the ideas she expounded? What of the teachings of DK? Where were they in my own life? Nowhere, it seemed. I had long since left the teachings behind. What interested me was Alice Bailey the historical figure and her achievements. I was especially motivated by my own outrage over the way she had been shafted by history and felt determined to put the situation to rights.

On November 28, 2018, in the week after *The Unlikely Occultist* was published, Steven Chernikeeff, founder of

Twelves and host of the 'Blavatsky Bailey Roerich' Facebook group, came across me on Goodreads. He left a comment on a review of my book. I came across the comment five days later. Who was this stranger with strong opinions? I felt compelled to respond. He must have liked my response as he replied straight away and then invited me to join his BBR Facebook group and share a link to *The Unlikely Occultist*. That was definitely not an opportunity an author passes up. Out of authorly politeness, I also bought his book *Esoteric Apprentice*.

I sensed from the outset that I needed to be very careful how I eased myself into the BBR milieu. I had no idea who anyone was or how the various strands of the theosophical scene fitted together, but I did know that my impulsive nature and wild enthusiasm can be off-putting. I have never forgotten a day back in 1982 when I overheard a friend describe me as a steamroller. Ouch!

When I joined BBR in 2018, I knew no one from the Bailey community other than Viv and Judy of Sydney Goodwill who were very lovely and supportive during my PhD years. I had heard of a few names like Dot Maver, Nancy Roof and Vita de Waal. I gained the impression from my research that there was a sort of dynasty at play in the dominant organisations. I also knew I needed to present myself well in Chernikeeff's Facebook group and, given that I had penned a biographical novel of Alice Bailey, I would be watched and judged. I was also in awe of everyone. I stepped into this wondrous new reality and suddenly I was exposed to all kinds of activities and people I had absolutely no idea existed.

I had walked the path of the outlier, adopting a stance of non-participation since the early 1990s when I found and then left the Arcane School. After joining BBR, I decided there would be no more dabbling at the edges for me, and I have tried to be true to my word ever since.

Before long, Steven encouraged me to join Twelves and I did. Lifelong theosophist Patrick Chouinard befriended me soon after. I worked with another highly respected theosophist, Murray Stentiford, to build the Twelves website. I met others, very welcoming men and women, some of whom I felt especially connected to.

Friendship bonds among those with a shared spiritual outlook are often deep and strong. It is a friendship like no other. I often find myself chatting on the phone or online to my soul-pals for hours at a time, and I love connecting with fellow travellers. Whether I like it or not, I belong. Whether I rail against it sometimes, I belong. Whether I want to run away somewhere else and have a go at being ordinary, I cannot leave this otherworld. The door won't close.

Not long into our friendship, Steven urged me to write a non-fiction biography of Alice Bailey and after some months of resisting the very idea, I re-entered the world of research and went on to work twelve-hour days, seven days a week, for months writing the new version. I worked furiously as there was a sense that the book needed to be out by the Full Moon of May (Wesak) 2020, Wesak being a significant date in the Bailey calendar. A couple of chapters were set to be highly controversial and because of that, the composition of the whole book had an edgy, charged feel. Also, I felt the weight of judgement, the scrutiny my words would receive. It was a huge responsibility and a huge undertaking and I only managed to write the book so fast because I had already written much of the content a few years earlier.

I am glad I worked that intensively, and I am glad I did bring the book to fruition in a crushingly short timeframe, but it did come with its own problems. There were corrections to be made. And, as anticipated, the book upset some prominent figures. I faced months of acrimony and made additional changes to appease. Cruel words were written about and to me, and threats were made that echoed events in my past. After many months of opposition, I wanted to shut the door on the Bailey community, block Alice Bailey from my life, and devote the rest of my days to writing fiction. I felt at odds with myself. I knew I still had work to do, obligations to fulfil. I couldn't just walk away. But I was simply too hurt and needed time to recover.

I think of human beings as a confluence of energies, merging and influencing, exerting pressure to do and be. I was wrestling with my reactions, not least shock and disbelief that I found myself in that horrible situation, a situation largely of my own making, and at the same time I was re-evaluating my sense of belonging, and trying to decide what it was that was required of me next.

I left Twelves during that time, and rejoined in 2021. Both times, I became immersed in Twelves, in its language and protocols, and the daily and weekly rhythm of the meditations. I came to believe the Twelves group marks a special moment in the history of the Bailey movement and in esoteric practice. Twelves is pure white magic in action. It is a condensation of all that Alice Bailey (and DK) taught, but it is more than that and has a different source.

I remain a steadfast supporter of Twelves. For an outsider like me, it isn't easy being a part of any group. I'm a very poor follower or participant of anything that requires me to commit to a set of ideas or beliefs. I have a tendency to see through and past language. I remain sceptical of metaphysics. I'm invested in an esoteric way of knowing which I also view as a kind of unknowing. I guess feeling puzzled and doubtful is just my way. In Twelves, I wear the wisdom like voile, not velvet, allowing the language to be see-through and therefore seen through as the words exert their influence. Twelves has shown me this, allowed me to understand this. What matters isn't the language but rather the doing or making things that are positive or good, acting in the world to make a difference. Twelves is esoteric praxis in its soulful guise and whatever I may think of this or that invocation, or this or that teaching, the source is pure as is the intent.

Through Twelves, I have come to realise that the esoteric teachings of DK and their Twelves counterpart The Initiate set a high but not unattainable bar. And that if you have an esoteric disposition, then Twelves represents the very best kind of esoteric work the world has to offer, one that appeals to those with a mystic as much as an esoteric disposition.

JOINING TWELVES

I first heard about Twelves in January 2019. At the time, founder Steven Chernikeeff was promoting his book, *Esoteric Apprentice*. When I inquired about Twelves, he advised me to read the book, so I plucked my copy off my bookshelf and opened to the first page.

Esoteric Apprentice charts the history of Twelves and its original group, formed in the 1980s. The group had an international membership but did manage to physically meet for the Twelves ritual. Back then, communication was by letter or landline. I found that alone impressive, just thinking of the logistics involved in bringing together twelve individuals from around the world.

Twelves evolved out of Steven's visits to Twelves cofounding member Robert Adams's meditation studio in London. Steven was an earnest young man, a seeker from an early age, first devouring the teachings of Spiritualism before migrating into Theosophy, and discovering the Bailey books and the Lucis Trust. Robert and Steven's late-night conversations and meditations in Robert's studio culminated at the stroke of midnight on New Year's Eve

1981, when Steven received a symbol and a message. The atmosphere in the shed that night was electric. In the months that followed, more instructions were received, along with an invitation 'to undertake work in Twelve Formation and to act as a conduit for Hierarchical ashramic energy'. The work had begun. Soon to join the duo was Dr Peter Maslin, a highly regarded Alice Bailey expert who became instrumental in helping administrate Twelves.

Between 1982 and 1986, Steven received teachings which would inform how Twelves functioned. For twenty years Twelves grew and members met annually to perform the core ritual. It was to be the stage of preparation, that stage eventually discontinuing, partly due to the passing of both Robert and Peter which left a vacuum at the core of the group, and partly because Steven's energies were increasingly focused on his other commitments.

Reading about this first phase of Twelves was inspiring. By the book's end I knew all about Twelves, its history and rationale, but I still knew nothing of Twelves. I had no direct knowledge and could only imagine from the outside what it might be like on the inside. I only knew that a new phase of Twelves work had begun and I was right there, almost at the start.

I told Steven I would like to join and then I had to wait. I have no idea why my initial raised hand received no response, but I persisted, mentioning it again a few weeks later. Still nothing.

I had to ask three times before the door opened and I went through a short induction and vetting process and was accepted.

I remember back then feeling in awe of Steven. He came across as focused, determined and a little impatient, and he didn't suffer fools. He would go head-to-head in heated discussions in his Facebook group, something that both impressed and scared me. He carried an air of intensity about him, and a passion and deep commitment that became more obvious the more I grew to know him. Research is second nature to me, and I discovered some things about Steven online that endeared him to me. He openly admits to growing up in an orphanage. And that his father's line comprises minor Russian aristocracy. Over the few years I have known him and after I earned his respect, a rapport has grown, a sense of shared purpose, and a sharp focus on the work at hand. I feel connected to Steven. He's like an older wiser sibling. Observing him navigate the steady evolution of Twelves, managing all of the relationship dynamics among core members, I cannot help but be impressed. He conducts himself with restraint, reins himself in, gives the organising group enough freedom and autonomy to conduct its affairs, and reaches out a steadying hand if things get wobbly, which they do from time to time. It's the nature of groups. He's very conscious of the way he conducts himself, very aware of the group. He also restrains his own ego, never letting his core position and unique connection to the ashram distort his sense of who he is and what he's purposed to do. There is nothing of the guru about Steven.

Back in 2019, joining Twelves meant I had entered another world, a world filled with lifelong meditators. *Who are these people? They are very nice but they all seem so very advanced.* I felt like an imposter (I still feel like an imposter). I had to battle fear and uncertainty. I didn't want to let the group down. Despite having read *Esoteric Apprentice*, I was wondering who this Steven Chernikeeff really was and even if he could be trusted, or if any of what Twelves was doing was real or could harm me.

My service work up until I joined Twelves had been on the outer planes, and for decades I felt I needed to shut myself off from inner planes work because it shifts the perspective. I needed to stay focused in the mundane world to complete my work. That was my rationale. I just didn't seem to find it in me to switch in and out. I suppose on some level I feared losing my chosen sense of direction. Those first six months in Twelves I spent shilly-shallying. When it came to making time for the meditations, things weren't going that well for me. I stayed, for eighteen months I stayed, and I struggled the whole time.

What first attracted me to Twelves was the idea of harnessing the power of thought to make a positive difference in the world. Although Twelves doesn't so much harness thought as intention. And that intention aims to call upon, harness and then draw down spiritual energy; to act as a conduit so that this energy can more easily reach Earth, reach humanity, and influence hearts and minds. Meditations, which are really rituals enacted through invocation and visualisation, are held in groups of twelve, that number providing strength and resilience and protection.

Twelves is grounded in the theosophical current of esoteric thought. A keynote of Theosophy is the existence of a spiritual hierarchy of celestial beings dedicated to advancing the evolution of consciousness of humanity. For me, 'spiritual hierarchy' and 'the masters of the wisdom', is the language theosophists employ to describe intermediaries. If consciousness evolves, and I think it does, then these beings are a logical extension of the process. I can accept that much. But one of my difficulties being part of Twelves is that doubt is hardwired in me. Faith is not in my genes. I don't believe in anything. I am a supreme agnostic, especially when it comes to anything metaphysical. Even astrology, for which I have a natural ability, I doubt and question, always mindful of confirmation bias. Yet astrology as a symbolic temporal system is a mechanism for the generation of insight and through that insight, astrology does reveal or point the way, not of itself but rather through the interpretive lens of the astrologer, the supreme storyteller. Although a natal chart does portray, metaphorically, a life. It seems almost undeniable to anyone familiar with it. That sort of ambivalence and cautious acceptance is about as far as I am prepared to take the esoteric. As for the spiritual hierarchy, I just don't know.

The esoteric way of knowing involves recognising patterns and connections. And I have to admit that my birthdate has always held some significance, connecting me to my Spiritualist maternal grandmother and two other relatives. This feeling was reinforced when I discovered the Sabian symbols which were devised by leading astrologer Marc Edmund Jones from clairvoyant Elsie Wheeler's visions of each of 360 white cards, cards which, unbeknown to her, denoted the degrees of the zodiac. The system was later developed by renowned astrologer Dane Rudhyar. When I turned to the symbol for my birthdate, I had a surprise. *A secret meeting of men responsible for executive decisions in world affairs.* Esoterically this refers to an inner government or 'occult Hierarchy', the 'White Lodge'. I have thought ever since that denying the existence of the spiritual hierarchy was perhaps tantamount to denying, on some level and in some small way, my own existence.

These intersections of time and symbol, these so-called coincidences, have to mean *something* to an esotericist. That's the whole point.

The reader will be now be thinking, how can this Doubting Thomas of a human whose esoteric credentials are at best questionable find herself in Twelves? I could refer to Pascal's Wager, which, after all, is a valid option when it comes to accepting the existence of God.

And after joining Twelves, I took on a form of that wager. It's the best I could do. One thing I do know is that there exists some ineffable reality beyond the human senses that cannot be explained away by pure chance. The only evidence I have for the existence of this reality is the way my own life has unfolded. The way Alice Bailey came to literally fall into my hands in the form of one of her books. The way I found myself studying the Bailey books for my PhD which was never my intention. The way critical events and happenstances pile up at key moments, marking major turning points, as if life itself is conspiring to push me in a fresh direction. The way I am drawn in, like an iron filing, to the very theosophical teachings I so often question. There is a part of me that connects, a part of me hidden from my own view that steers my life, sets before me certain tasks, introduces me to key people. And I have come to accept that whoever this other me is, she is worth listening to, worth obeying, even if it means the rest of me is sometimes dragged kicking and screaming as I fulfil some special task. That said, I make no pretensions of being anything other than an ordinary human being who has striven to be the best version of herself possible, and who loves writing novels, watching Netflix and going for long walks. A writer who made a commitment to being a part of Twelves.

At the heart of Twelves is a commitment not only to the spiritual hierarchy but its externalisation. By externalisation is meant a visible physical manifestation, or 'the unveiling of those at the heart of human evolution'.

When talking of externalising and unveiling, it isn't that a curtain on a grand stage is suddenly going to part and there they all are, bowing for the applause. The process occurs in the hearts and minds of us as we begin to recognise their existence. And it isn't that vast numbers of us will suddenly look up, our faces filled with awe. The process of recognition will likely be subtle. But that's just my view.

A second commitment, one that forms the lifeblood of

Twelves, is the upcoming conclave of the Spiritual Hierarchy scheduled for Wesak, May 2025, when it is predicted in the Bailey books that humanity's fate will be decided and the externalisation process can start to unfold in the following decade. Twelves is working towards and beyond that pivotal date to enable a sort of supercharging of the spiritualisation of humanity. When it comes to these central tenets of Twelves, I again apply Pascal's Wager, as I continue to harbour ambivalence and doubt and know I will never be a fully-fledged adherent to any metaphysical system despite being profoundly drawn to the 'world of meaning'. And in the words of Patrick Chouinard:

 I've always liked the saying 'normal is over-rated'. This is the dawning of the Age of Aquarius as the song says, and if we can get through the next few years things are going to get a lot weirder (as HPB [Blavatsky] predicted) but in a good way. I'm an optimist – though it's hard at times – but I think we need to be, because energy follows thought. Even DK says that souls with gifts we can scarcely imagine are incarnating and will do so increasingly – bringing solutions to many problems. A magical age is beginning and Twelves is magical work.

NUMBERS AND YEARS: 12 AND 2025

 $\mathcal{C}$ entral to Twelves is a number and a date: 12 and 2025. Performing a ritual in a group of Twelve is based on sound occult reasoning, the number itself known for its strength.

Since ancient times, number has had an occult aspect, each numeral from one to twelve carrying its own measure of significance. Divisible by 2, 3, 4 and 6, 12 itself is thought to be the number of completion. Down the ages, the number twelve has also been fundamental to key areas of human society.

In timekeeping, there are twelve hours in the day and night, and twelve months in the year. Before metrification, twelve was the key division of measurement, the duodecimal system. In law, there are today twelve jurors. In the world of religion, there are twelve prophets, the twelve patriarchs, the twelve tribes, the twelve followers of Buddha, the Twelve Adityas in Hinduism, the twelve petals of the Anahata Chakra, and the twelve Apostles of Christianity. In the Bible, in the Book of Revelation and elsewhere, the number twelve, and its perfect square 144, are mentioned many times. In speaking of the New

Jerusalem: 'It had a great high wall, with twelve gates, and at the gates, twelve angels; and names were written on them, which are the names of the twelve tribes of the sons of Israel.' Revelation 21:12

In mythology there were Twelve Knights of the Round Table, Twelve Olympian Gods in the Greek Pantheon, the Twelve Great Gods of Egypt, Twelve followers of Quetzacoatl, and the Twelve Labours of Hercules. In esotericism, there are the twelve masonic signs of recognition. And developed out of the twelve-pointed star is the archeometre, an instrument for predicting events and coordinating knowledge.

Then there are the twelve signs of the zodiac. For the Zoroastrians, the zodiacal signs are the Twelve Commanders on the side of Light. The signs are formed out of the four elements of earth, air, water and fire, in combination with their three successive states of evolution, to form a complete whole.

For Steven Chernikeeff, the number twelve is 'the magical number that works in complete harmony with nature, the earth, and the cosmos'.[1]

Esoteric rituals down the ages have always begun with the creation of a circle of protection, a sacred circle that both contains all held within and forms a barrier to any unwelcome force or entity from without. A circle forms a continuous line that can accommodate the formation of triangles and star formations. Some formations are stronger than others and twelve, or four sets of three triangles, is especially strong and enabling when drawing on spiritual and sacred energies in magical work. A Twelve Formation is comprised of four triangles, the most basic of two-dimensional formations, and those triangles also form for squares within the circle, locking participants into a tightly connected framework, a strong boundary that can withstand forces from without and energies within.

ON THE YEAR 2025

A condensed version of this chapter appears in the May/June 2020 edition of New Dawn Magazine.

In Theosophy, the year 2025 is thought to mark a transition, a point in human history demanding radical change and even spiritual intervention to save us, largely from ourselves. So important is this year marking a turning point in human history that Twelves would probably not exist without it, at least not in this current guise. Fully understanding and embracing Twelves cannot be achieved without a solid sense of this turning point.

Until recently, many in the Western world would be forgiven for believing that the end-of-days narrative passed with the millennium since we have made it this far and we're still here. To maintain credibility, doomsday cults would need to revise their narratives. Yet as the first century of the new millennium enters its second decade, many may be beginning to wonder if the end-of-days timing wasn't a little bit off. After all, predictions made centuries ago might be regarded somewhat unreliable when it comes to exactitude.

The predictions of French astrologer and seer Nostradamus, who saw the end of the millennium as a period of much trauma and transition, was revised by some in the face of the Covid 19 pandemic and little wonder as nations went into lockdown. This novel coronavirus is surely a 'great plague' and it could arguably have begun in a 'maritime city' if we are prepared to bend the prediction to refer to Wuhan's wet food market.

The last years have also borne witness to extreme weather events besetting the planet including the apocalyptic Australian bushfires, the vicious storms and widespread flooding seen in Europe, and plagues of locusts of Biblical proportions in East Africa. At the time of writing, war rages in Ukraine. As our catastrophic times continue, showing no sign of abating, some are also anticipating planetary annihilation through an asteroid strike, predicted in the Book of Revelation. The dystopian among us have every reason to be worried. Situate current events against a backdrop of extreme global inequality with the top percentage of individuals and corporations holding an ever-increasing slice of wealth in a globalised world, and whatever cause we give to each individual catastrophe, our global situation appears in dire need of a reset.

KALI YUGA

It isn't just Nostradamus and the doomsday cults who have been predicting the turbulence and possible end of days humanity is currently experiencing. A current of thought within the Western esoteric tradition asserts humanity is exiting an old cycle and entering a new, and while for some this transition augurs a Golden Age, for others the potential for mass destruction is ever present.

Esotericism tends to hold fast to the belief that history is profoundly influenced if not determined by certain cosmic laws, by the movement of the planets, and by the intentions or aims and objectives of higher beings. Astrologers rely on the precession of equinoxes to denote the astrological ages, occurring in approximate chunks of two-thousand years and including the outgoing Age of Pisces and the incoming Age of Aquarius. Eastern mysticism looks to the four ages or yugas, the Hindu tradition situating humanity within the Kali Yuga or Dark Age which began in 3102 BCE and is set to endure for another 432,000 years.[2] The Kali Yuga is the most difficult and challenging of all the ages, noted for its harshness and intensity. It is an age many would be yearning to see the back of. After the Kali Yuga will come a new Krita/Satya

Yuga or Golden Age, but in the Hindu orthodoxy, we would have a long time to wait for its arrival.

In the 1900s, Western esotericists in the Traditionalist stream decided the epochal scale found in the Hindu Puranas much too large and surmised they had been deliberately given to mislead. As scholar Joscelyn Godwin notes, the Traditionalists revised calculations based on ratios and came up with three possible dates for the ending of the Kali Yuga. For Rene Guénon (1886-1951), the end date was 2000. Whereas Orientalist Alain Daniélou (1907-1994) decided humanity will have vanished from earth by 2442.[3]

Independently of the yuga cycles, French essayist and Traditionalist Gaston Georgel (1899-1988) affirmed the governing of history 'by cycles of 540, 1080 and 2160 years', noting a corresponding cyclic nature of historical events. After corresponding with Guénon who introduced him to his view of the Kali Yuga, Georgel placed the end of the cycle at around 2029-30.[4]

If Georgel's timescale is accepted, approaching fast and almost upon us is the possibility of a future Golden Age. But the Kali Yuga cycle was not thought to come to an end quietly. Georgel observed that during the last six hundred years of this outgoing Age, humanity has endured dictators and tyrannical states.

To prove their hypothesis that the dates given in the Puranas were vastly exaggerated, and that there was much value in observing how the astrological cycles play out in history and that their mathematical reconfigurations were accurate, the Traditionalists set about finding evidence. Guénon soon found Georgel's calculations to coincide remarkably well with key events, including the French and English revolutions.[5]

Independent researcher and writer Bibhu Dev Misra's calculations have brought the end date of the Kali Yuga forward a few years to 2025. For Misra, 'for the past 2,700 years we have been evolving through the ascending Kali Yuga', and the end of this Dark Age will 'inevitably be followed by cataclysmic earth changes and civilisation collapses, as is characteristic of the transitional periods'.[6] He notes a 'current upswing in tectonic activities and the increased incidence of extreme weather phenomena' as possible evidence of increasing volatility. 'We need to be aware of these greater cycles of time that govern human civilisation, and the changes that are looming in the horizon'.[7]

THEOSOPHY AND CYCLES

Among esotericists, it was not only the Traditionalists who turned to the East for inspiration of epochal cycles. Occultist and Russian aristocrat Madame Helena Petrovna Blavatsky incorporated the yugas into her conception of the root races, of which she wrote extensively.[8] Whether regarded as literal truth or metaphor, in Blavatsky's scheme a root race endures for over eight million years and spans two maha-yugas, or two cycles of the four Yugas. Along with these great cycles are numerous minor cycles associated with various races and nation states. A new root race emerges as the old one is finishing its second Kali Yuga age. In *The Secret Doctrine*, Blavatsky notes that the fourth sub-race of the Atlanteans were destroyed during its Kali Yuga. The Aryan race is now in its Kali Yuga, and will reap the fruits of its own doing as the incoming sixth sub-race begins its Satya Yuga or Golden Age.[9] The question remains as to whether humanity has learned its lessons from its Atlantean days and evolved sufficiently to be worthy of saving this time around.

THE MAHATMAS

The Theosophical Society was founded in New York in 1875 by Blavatsky (1831-91), lawyer and journalist Colonel Henry Steel Olcott (1832-1907), and Anglo-Irish mystic William Quan Judge (1851-96). The trio shared a prior interest in Spiritualism, with its belief in life after death and the ability, through the role of a medium, to contact and receive messages from the spirit world. Dissatisfied with both Spiritualism and Christianity, Blavatsky turned to the East for inspiration in order to revive an ancient and universal esoteric wisdom.

The ancient wisdom tradition, which can be traced back thousands of years, has its roots in contemporary Western thinking among the Greek philosophers including Plato, and in the East among Hindu sages. Blavatsky's Theosophy is underpinned by Hermetic philosophy adopted by the Neoplatonists of Late Antiquity. Theosophy is pantheistic, believing in a Divine Principle or Source from which All emanates and eventually Returns.

As noted above, a keynote of Western esotericism (and Eastern mysticism) is the transmission of wisdom passed on from master to disciple. Often this master would be physically present to the disciple. Central to Blavatsky's version of Theosophy is the existence of advanced beings or adepts, humans who have evolved to an advanced spiritual level, which she eventually termed Mahatmas. It was one such Mahatma, Morya, who is said to have communicated much of the material that comprises her seminal texts *Isis Unveiled* and *The Secret Doctrine*.

For theosophists, these adepts or Mahatmas form a secret brotherhood overseeing the evolution of humanity. They are simply a logical progression along the evolutionary path back to the Source. Blavatsky was keen to distance the Mahatmas from the entities found in the spirit world and contacted by mediums in séances, central to Spiritualist practice.

> Great are the desecrations to which the names of two of the masters have been subjected. There is hardly a medium who has not claimed to have seen them. Every bogus swindling Society, for commercial purposes, now claims to be guided and directed by 'masters,' often supposed to be far higher than ours![10]

Blavatsky, believed that the transition from the outgoing fifth or Aryan root race and the incarnating of the sixth root race would be marked by the appearance of the Maitreya, a messianic Mahayana Buddhist figure said to succeed the present Buddha. In the Buddhist tradition, the Maitreya will teach enlightenment in the coming age.

THE WORLD TEACHER

The belief that the Kali Yuga and the current root race are due to give way to a new Golden Age and root race, a transition inaugurated by the appearance of the Maitreya, evolved through the thinking of second-generation Theosophists Charles Webster Leadbeater (1854-1934) and Annie Besant (1847-1933). Blavatsky wrote of the Christ Principle, the idea that there exists inside of every human being a spiritual essence waiting to be awakened. Leadbeater went on to unite the idea of the Christ Principle with the Maitreya to form the by then much anticipated World Teacher. According to Leadbeater, the Maitreya had already incarnated in Atlantis, Ancient Egypt and Ancient India, and as Jesus Christ.[11]

Annie Besant was convinced the approach of the World Teacher was imminent and this became her main focus during her presidency of the Theosophical Society. In 1909 Leadbeater homed in on an Indian boy in the grounds of the society's headquarters in Adyar, India and, using his clairvoyant abilities, pronounced him to be the World Teacher.

Leadbeater and Annie Besant named the boy Jiddu Krishnamurti (1895-1986) and proceeded to prepare him for his future. The Order of the Star in the East was formed in 1911 with the fourteen-year-old Krishnamurti as the head, an organisation that attracted a membership of around 100,000 before it was dissolved in 1929. The activities of Besant and Leadbeater regarding Krishnamurti resulted in widespread condemnation and ridicule within the theosophical society. Krishnamurti went on to assume the role of a spiritual teacher, but without the grandiose status of World Teacher which he renounced in 1929, distancing himself from the whole project from then on.

ALICE BAILEY'S CHRISTOLOGY AND THE REAPPEARANCE OF THE CHRIST

The yugas or vast epochs based on the Hindu Puranas are not the only cycles to be found in Theosophical literature. As Georgel observed, the emerging Krita Yuga or Golden Age in the revised scheme proposed by the Traditionalists broadly coincides in its inception with the new age of Aquarius.

This astrological cycle based on the precession of equinoxes lasts 2160 years. The outgoing Age of Pisces is thought to have commenced in the century prior to the transition into the Common Era two-thousand years ago, which means the next age is due to begin soon, to be preceded by a two-hundred-year period of transition with Aquarian influences would begin to be felt. Astrologers do not agree on the exact timing largely due to the different sizes of the constellations of the zodiac. What matters is the universal agreement that humanity is undergoing a transition into a new age.

No esotericist embraced this concept of the dawning of a New Age of Aquarius more fully than Alice A. Bailey who contributed more than any other theorist to the emergence of the New Age movement. Some of the very first writings Bailey took down for the Tibetan comprise a delineation of the work of the Spiritual Hierarchy. The founding of the hierarchy, its structure and organisation, along with its purpose to serve as a guiding principle in the evolution of consciousness of humanity are all detailed in four chapters of *Initiation, Human and Solar*.

In this presentation, the Planetary Hierarchy has three departments corresponding to one of the three major rays: the will aspect, the love-wisdom aspect and the intelligence aspect.[12] Of concern for Bailey is the second aspect of love-wisdom, a department headed by the Christ or World Teacher who 'directs that indwelling consciousness in its life or spirit aspect, seeking to energise it within the form so that, in due course of time, that form can be discarded and the liberated spirit return whence it came.'[13]

Like her contemporaries Leadbeater and Besant, Bailey wholeheartedly believed in the reappearance of the Christ or World Teacher who would inaugurate a New Age of spiritual enlightenment, and His appearance would coincide with the start of the Golden Age of the yugas along with Blavatsky's root race transition, occurring around 2025. Bailey effectively pushed forward the timing of the World Teacher's appearance by a hundred years, distancing herself from the Krishnamurti debacle.

Bailey's Spiritual Hierarchy meets periodically to discuss world affairs, holding a centennial conclave to assess the evolutionary progress of humanity and decide on ways forward, including its own externalisation on earth. The last conclave took place in 1925 and oversaw a departmental reshuffle in preparation.

> The steps taken at the Conclave in Shamballa in 1925 (based on tentative conclusion at the previous centennial Conclave) and the pressures exerted by the Hierarchy have proved most successful, and out of the chaos of the world war (precipitated by humanity itself) there is developing a structure of truth and a paralleling responsiveness of the human mechanism which guarantees the perpetuation and the rapid unfoldment of the next stage of the teaching of the Ageless Wisdom.[14]

Referring back to the Kali Yuga period of the Atlantean root race, in the Bailey texts, Djwhal Khul claims the Hierarchy withdrew 'behind the separating curtain' marking a long 'interlude of darkness, of aridity and a cycle of 'blank abstraction,' which persisted in its crudest form until 1425 A.D., and since then has sensibly lightened until we reached the year 1925.'[15]

The previous centennial conclave of 1925 puts Alice Bailey's own organisations at the fulcrum of change. Particularly when, as part of the Hierarchy's outreach program, the New Group of World Servers was formed in the early 1930s, comprising aspirants and disciples who were largely students of Alice Bailey's Arcane School or otherwise studying the teachings. It might also be no accident that Alice Bailey's *A Treatise on Cosmic Fire*, the psychological key to *The Secret Doctrine*, was published in 1925.[16] This then, became an integral part of a new Plan for humanity.

> This Plan was tentatively formulated in 1900, at one of the great quarterly meetings of the Hierarchy. In 1925...members of that important Council determined two things: First, that there should be a united effort by the collective members of the planetary Hierarchy...to bring about certain definite results, and that during that time the attention of the Great Ones should be turned towards a definite attempt to expand the consciousness of humanity and to institute a sort of forcing process...Secondly, it was determined to link more closely and subjectively the senior disciples, aspirants and workers in the world... Thus the New Group of World Servers came into being.[17]

Within this esoteric thoughtform, the New Group of World Servers has quickened the approach of the Hierarchy through various endeavours including World Goodwill, Triangles and Full Moon meditations all designed to pour light into the world. There is no detail in the texts of the contributions of other spiritual groups who do not subscribe to the Bailey model.

While the Bailey movement cannot be regarded insular or exclusive, there exists nevertheless a very particular charge or responsibility placed on the shoulders of followers to gather their forces and help advance the cause. A Christian by nature if not always by creed, Bailey never lost her missionary zeal. It might be argued she was the perfect fit for the objectives of the Hierarchy. Conversely, others may accuse her of taking traditional theosophical ideas and shaping them to suit her own ambitions.

Of greater import still is the question of truth. Is any of

this real? Do the yugas exist? What of the root races? And what of a Great White Lodge of more spiritually advanced humans? In Bailey's model, we are not being governed solely by cycles and deciding the validity of these cycles through the esoteric art of correspondence, we are being told by an authoritative figure via a messenger who may or may not be trusted.

As mentioned above, intermediaries, whether angels, spirits or mythical figures, are not new to esotericism. Yet the assertion that these intermediaries are an inner government exerting influence on world affairs might be hard for some to swallow.

Bailey composed much of her opus during turbulent times. As the 1930s shaded into the 1940s, it became clear all was not rosy for the New Group of World Servers, or indeed, for just about anyone else. In a newsletter distributed to the group on April 1943, Djwhal Khul hints at the approach of the Hierarchy but all is far from guaranteed.

66 Much however depends upon the aspirants and the disciples in the world at this time. The past year has been one of the world's worst experiences from the standpoint of agony and distress; the point of acutest suffering has been reached. It has, however, been the year in which the greatest spiritual Approach of all time has shown itself to be possible—an Approach for which the initiates and Masters have for centuries been preparing, and for which all the Wesak Festivals since the meeting of the Great Council in 1925 have been preparatory.[18]

For Bailey, since 1925, humanity has been receiving

hierarchical stimulation, allowing in the light and inflowing Christ principle of brotherhood and goodwill, and slowly awakening the masses. Throughout the later texts, there is a sense of tremendous uplifting and hope that despite the horrors of the Second World War, humanity faces a bright and positive future not too far off.

Whether Bailey is right, the New Age movement most certainly did come into being, for better or worse depending on your point of view, and took its shape largely due to the Bailey teachings and associated movement, and new ideas of interconnectedness, unity or wholeness, and inclusiveness central to the Bailey teachings have certainly found expression in a variety of ways. But any hoped-for global utopia has not yet manifested. Far from it. Many would argue dystopia is manifesting in its stead.

THE 2025 CONCLAVE OF THE SPIRITUAL HIERARCHY

The Bailey teachings were given in the period from 1918 to 1949 when Alice Bailey died, in preparation for the next conclave of the Spiritual Hierarchy in 2025, after which a third outpouring from the Masters of the Wisdom is predicted to occur and the Bailey teachings will be superseded. Adherents are firm in their belief that these dates, give or take a year, are accurate. There is growing anticipation within the Bailey community as we enter the five-year period prior to the conclave, something akin to a quickening. Optimism and hope are prevalent and yet some are highlighting a rather worrying caveat Djwhal Khul made clear in the Bailey texts. It turns out the hierarchy has placed some conditions upon its return. If in the 2025 conclave it is decided that humanity has not met these conditions, then the hierarchy will in effect wash its hands of us and humanity will be destroyed. It is not the masters who are going to destroy humanity. Rather, they will withdraw, no doubt leaving humanity to destroy itself. The three conditions are couched in obscure terms.

> Above everything else required at this time is a recognition of the world of meaning, a recognition of Those Who implement world affairs and Who engineer those steps which lead mankind onward towards its destined goal, plus a steadily increased recognition of the Plan on the part of the masses.[19]

In other words, humanity, or at least those reading the Bailey books, are already to have gained a measure of the esoteric sense, the ability to cut away illusion and delusion by looking beneath the surface of things, both through interpreting situations metaphorically and symbolically, and through developing the intuition to penetrate a deeper occult or causal reality, the realm of the soul. The esoteric sense is a way of perceiving:

> Esoteric study, when coupled with esoteric living, reveals in time the world of meaning and leads eventually to the world of significances. The esotericist starts by endeavouring to discover the reason why; he wrestles with the problem of happenings, events, crises and circumstances in order to arrive at the meaning.[20]
>
> He thus acquires entrance into the world of meaning. Events, circumstances, happenings and physical phenomena of every kind are simply symbols of what is occurring in the inner worlds.[21]

Along with a recognition of the world of meaning, there needs to be a widespread acknowledgement and acceptance of the existence of the spiritual hierarchy or inner government overseeing world affairs. The masses in large part are to recognise, however dimly, that a spiritual plan for humanity exists.

What evidence is there that any other portion of humanity has ticked these criteria? Does it even matter? To the Bailey community, it does. And the Bailey books offer a stark warning.

> These three recognitions must be evidenced by humanity and affect human thinking and action if the total destruction of mankind is to be averted. They must form the theme of all the propaganda work to be done during the next few decades—until the year 2025—a brief space of time indeed to produce fundamental changes in human thought, awareness, and direction, but—at the same time— a quite possible achievement, provided the New Group of World Servers and the men and women of goodwill perform a conscientious task. Evil is not yet sealed.[22]

Do the extremes of pandemic, war, fire and flood represent just the beginning of a long series of cataclysms? Does this mark the end of the Kali Yuga, going out with a bang style? All of these catastrophes are a consequence of our own behaviour, as humanity continues along unsustainable paths of overpopulation, a contentious topic for some, and destruction of environments. For the Bailey community each event is also an opportunity for humanity to rise up together as one, through myriad small and large acts of goodwill and sacrifice, laying the ground for the reappearance of the World Teacher in whatever form that might take.

As national governments grapple with the economic and health crises created by Covid 19, and as they look to each other and strive to agree on an international response not seen since World War Two as Alice Bailey came to the end of her writing journey with the Tibetan, Djwhal Khul, perhaps we are seeing emerging something along the following lines:

> The inner structure of the World Federation of Nations will eventually be equally well organised, with its outer form taking rapid shape by 2025. Do not infer from this that we shall have a perfected world religion and a complete community of nations. Not so rapidly does nature move; but the concept and the idea will be universally recognised, universally desired, and generally worked for, and when these conditions exist nothing can stop the appearance of the ultimate physical form for that cycle.[23]

Is this, an 'intensification of the light' predicted by Djwhal Khul back in the 1930s and set to 'continue until 2025', in which 'the soul will be recognised as a fact'?[24] The Bailey teachings are peppered lightly with references to 2025 and liberally with the notion of the reappearance of the World Teacher. 'Thus, a great and new movement is proceeding and a tremendously increased interplay and interaction is taking place. This will go on until A.D. 2025.'[25] Everything Alice Bailey was putting into place, 'as regards the particular planning with which we are dealing, is from now until the year 2025 A.D.'.[26]

A leading voice in the build-up to the 2025 conclave,

Steven Chernikeeff anticipates a 'great upheaval' involving 'huge environmental changes, magnetic activity (including the shifting of the Pole), disasters, political upheavals and wars'.[27]

Twelves is an exemplar of the efforts esotericists and mystics are making to ward off cataclysm and usher in a better era. That Twelves currently enjoys a pronounced upswing in activity as more and more are seeking to create a bridge to the hierarchy in order to drawn down the spiritual energies, demonstrates the depth of commitment and dedication to make spiritual change a reality.

---

1. Chernikeeff, *Esoteric Apprentice*, p.43
2. see Glenn Kreisberg (ed.), Mysteries of the Ancient Past: A Graham Hancock Reader (Rochester: Bear & Co, 2012).
3. Joscelyn Godwin, 'When Does the Kali Yuga End?' New Dawn Magazine 138 (May-June 2013)
4. Ibid.; and Pierre A. Riffard, 'The Esoteric Method' in Antoine Faivre & Wouter J. Hanegraaff (eds.), Western Esotericism and the Science of Religion (Leuven: Peeters, 1998), 66.
5. Joscelyn Godwin, op. cit.
6. Bibhu Dev Misra, 'The end of the Kali Yuga in 2025: Unraveling the Mysteries of the Yuga Cycle'. Graham Hancock 15 July 2012, cited 29 March 2020. <https://grahamhancock.com/dmisrab6/>
7. Ibid.
8. See Joscelyn Godwin, 'Blavatsky and the First Generation of Theosophy' in Olav Hammer and Mikael Rothstein (eds.) *Handbook of the Theosophical Current* (Leiden: Brill, 2013) 13-31.
9. Helena P. Blavatsky, The Secret Doctrine Vol II, 147.
10. Helena P. Blavatsky, The Key to Theosophy (Pasadena: Theosophical University Press, 1972), 301-3.
11. See Annie Besant &Charles W. Leadbeater, *Man: How, Whence, and Whither; a record of clairvoyant investigation*. (Adyar, India: Theosophical Publishing House, 1913), 339 and 520; and
    Charles Leadbeater, *The Masters and the Path*. New York: Cosimo Classics, 2007), 278.
12. The rays – there are seven in all – are a theosophical re-languaging of Neoplatonic emanationism.
    Alice A. Bailey, Initiation, Human and Solar (New York, Lucis Trust, 1992), 44.
13. Ibid.

14. Alice A. Bailey *Discipleship in the New Age Vol II* (New York: Lucis Trust, 1986), 314.
15. Bailey, *Discipleship Vol II,* 316.
16. Alice A. Bailey, *The Unfinished Autobiography* (New York: Lucis Trust, 1951), 214.
17. Alice A. Bailey, *Esoteric Psychology Vol 1* (New York: Lucis Trust, 1971),170.
18. Alice A. Bailey, *The Externalisation of the Hierarchy,* (New York: Lucis Trust, 1957), 389.
19. Bailey, *Discipleship Vol II,* 164.
20. Alice A. Bailey, Education in the New Age (New York: Lucis Trust, 1954), 66.
21. Ibid., 62.
22. Bailey, *Discipleship Vol II,* 164.
23. Bailey, *Esoteric Psychology Vol 1,* 177.
24. bid., 103.
25. Alice Bailey, *The Externalisation,* 530.
26. Ibid., 562.
27. Steven Chernikeeff, *Esoteric Apprentice* (BBR Publications, 2018), 162.

CREATING THE
FOUNDATIONS FOR TWELVES

*W*hen I joined Twelves in early 2019 the group comprised about twenty members who communicated via a group Messenger chat. Gradually, others joined, and some left after finding the group wasn't for them. The atmosphere was tentative. No one knew if this current incarnation of Twelves would succeed. Hope was the driving force, hope that the group would expand and realise the goal of finding 144 dedicated disciples to work in a formation of twelve groups of twelve by 2025. To give an idea of those early days, here is a summary from Steven posted to the group:

 Hi everyone, let's sum up:
> We continue Twelves (obviously) at FM
> We continue Triangles
> We continue TAMs at weekends for those that wish to join - many of us actually do TAMs at other times too, when convenient, and everyone is welcome to add to that effort at any time

We agree that a Zoom TAM at the mid-point weekend between FM's is a positive contribution and we will experiment with building a TAM/Twelve connection at these times

In other words... a mid-FM TAM that will seek to build on the TAMs we have been doing but... with an added Twelve Formation as we move into the first 'Wall of Light'. As stated this will give everyone a 'flavour' of Twelves - bit of an experiment. We will be launching more Twelves, with focus, later this year/early 2020. We intend to undertake Ray Work, City Work, Antahkarana Work and work with the political sector (non-partisan). In addition to this we will be doing thoughtform building and, more carefully, thoughtform destroying. More about this nearer the 'time'.

Steven Chernikeeff

THE INTENTION of forming a single group of Twelve to perform the Twelves ritual meditation was yet to be realized. While we waited for enough members and figured out as a group how things would work, members formed Triangles – the very basic unit of group formation practicing a daily ritual. Triangles was founded by Alice Bailey in the 1920s and practiced by Bailey students the world over.

Finding myself doing a daily Triangles meditation felt strange at first. The ritual was something I had known about for decades and never engaged in as I didn't see it for what it is, esoteric work, and I rather cynically decided it wouldn't do any good anyway so I ignored it. As a member of Twelves, I had to push aside my prejudices and false opinions. I soon found the technique personally stabilising and surprisingly potent.

TRIANGLES

Using the Great Invocation (see below), groups of three visualize energies of light and goodwill circulating through the three focal points of their triangle. These energies pour out through the network of triangles surrounding the planet. Participants then imagine the hearts and minds of humanity irradiated with these energies of light and goodwill, strengthening all that is good and true and beautiful in the world.

The Great Invocation

From the point of Light within the Mind of God
Let light stream forth into the minds of men.
Let Light descend on Earth.

From the point of Love within the Heart of God
Let love stream forth into the hearts of men.
May Christ return to Earth.

From the centre where the Will of God is known
Let purpose guide the little wills of men –
The purpose which the Masters know and serve.

From the centre which we call the race of men
Let the Plan of Love and Light work out
And may it seal the door where evil dwells.
Let Light and Love and Power restore the Plan on Earth.

In Twelves, members commit to performing the meditation at a time that suits them. Triangles typically consist of members spread across the globe, so time-coordinated meditations are tricky.

* * *

As the months passed, Steven began hosting The Ashram Meditation or TAM on Zoom, recording it for those who couldn't attend. I found factoring in this flexibility convenient. Sometimes I attended, sometimes I listened to the recording. TAMs were held intermittently, the Twelves group yet to establish a regular rhythm and they lasted for about forty minutes.

In a TAM, Steven guides participants through a series of circles of light, arriving at the heart of the Ashram. Invocations are recited, a visualisation conjuring a vortex of light. After some moments of stillness, participants are then guided back through the circles of light and the meditation ends.

It's a beautiful, simple moving to the heart of the Ashram, and to begin with, I underestimated its significance and importance. The TAM was presented as preparatory for the Twelves ritual, and I didn't really understand its potency. Connecting with the inner Ashram, that part of the spiritual hierarchy that guides and envelopes Twelves and provides the stimulatory ideas for its unfoldment, is vital essential work, priming participants, rendering them more effective.

Before a Twelves ritual could be held, a protocol was needed. As participants were spread around the world with little possibility of coming together, the term 'Distant Twelve' caught on. Here is the first protocol which was created before I joined Twelves:

DISTANT TWELVE PROTOCOL

When considering this work, it is useful to be reminded that Light, in the esoteric sense, carries with it Power and Love. Hence the last phrase of The Great Invocation:

LET Light and Love and Power restore the Plan on Earth

THIS TRIUNE ENERGY, combined, is the force which binds esoteric group work together and allows the New Group of World Servers[1] access to the higher points of energy to distribute to the Grid of Light in a purposeful and meaningful way. Our work together seeks to 'magnetise' the work of the NGWS to an even greater level than is possible in groups of three and reflect the perfection that is Cosmos.

A single Distant Twelve is more powerful than a single Triangle but much less than a physical Twelve.

Training in Triangles makes the transition to Twelves easier.

1. We prepare a large group of experienced coworkers to meet physically to undertake the advance white magic work that lays before us. This pool allows us more certainty that twelve will be available and ready and these may come from any of the Distant Twelves that we have set up.
2. You will learn, discover and participate in the group 'Note' as this pervades our work together. It is the Note of the ashram and so listen well

dear friend... for it tolls continually. Our OMs
will reflect it.

PROCESS

THERE ARE three stages to your welcomed participation:

1. Joining the Twelves 'pool' and being allocated a
   Triangle and undertaking your commitment to
   work in unison, at the times you agree, with
   your coworkers
2. After allocation to a Distant Twelve undertaking
   the participation outlined here
3. If possible seriously considering joining us
   physically when the time comes*
4. *this is not a requirement to joining a Distant
   Twelve but we would like to offer everyone that
   opportunity. We are currently considering
   Glastonbury, England or New York, USA as
   locations.

YOU WILL BE WELL VERSED in how a Triangle works and,
hopefully, establish good relations with your two
coworkers. It is now time to expand that, from January
Full Moon 2019, into a more focused intent. This work
should not be taken lightly, although we do enjoy a great
sense of humour and camaraderie in the group, as the
focus required can be intense especially at the later
stages when we undertake the active destruction and
creating of thoughtforms. Also active and direct contact
with our ashramic coworkers can have large impact on
each of us individually as well as a group. On the protec-

tion side you need have no fears as we act under the ashramic 'umbrella' and invoke that protection at all stages.

THE FOLLOWING IS A 'WORK-IN-PROGRESS' and may be subject to change and refinement as we progress the distant side to Twelves.

FIRST STAGE

This is an individual responsibility and apart from the obvious cautions about drugs, alcohol etc. not being in the 'mix' it is important for coworkers to be ready with 'intent'. That is to say preparing ones 'being' at least 3 days before a Twelve and requesting right action in your daily meditations and invocations. A calm, focused intent is required for this work and, most important, LEAVE your personal 'stuff' at the door when entering.

ASSUMING that you are now focused, trained in the art of Triangles, keep emotions and mental faculties under control have read and understood the *Esoteric Apprentice* (a requirement) and have understood that any other issues in your personal life have to be set aside whilst you undertake this service activity we can advance to Stage Two.

SECOND STAGE

Whenever I undertake group work I ask for protection and in a larger group setting such as the Twelves Work I recite The Great Invocation and I would advise you to do the same. All of your coworkers will be trained, focused and inter-changeable. You might find it helpful to visualise coworkers outlined and surrounded by light but not a specific person, male or female etc.

THIS PERSON VISUALISED REPRESENTS, and IS, one of your coworkers in the Triangle that is about to interlace with another three other Triangles. When the connection is firm recite The Great Invocation in anticipation of joining the larger group formation.

THIRD STAGE

When the time has come, ideally at the synchronised time but not a strict requirement, see your Triangle floating above the other three Triangles already in formation (nine) and sounding the OM lower your Triangle onto the Nine completing the Twelve.

WHEN YOU ARE ADVANCED in this work you will definitely feel the stages of connection and it is quite dramatic, occultly speaking, when the Triangles merge and the Twelve is complete. But this is the beginning as we are a battery only but if we are successful and connection with the ashram is made, I must emphasise, BY THE GROUP as a unit then the anticipatory buildup of energy is palpable and, on occasion, seen.

DO NOT BE SURPRISED, in your daily life, if things start to 'happen' and a feeling of being 'full of energy' (as occultly understood) is with you in surprising ways. It is life changing, if properly applied, and I have always described it as a magnet. One end is self and the other is the ashram and once that has been established it 'pulls' you. I'm sure many of you will have felt this in other esoteric work but it really intensifies with advanced group white magic work. Do not be alarmed! Hidden hands guide us.

FOURTH STAGE

Now the connection is made. Visualise your eleven coworkers in formation. Recite again The Great Invocation followed by three OMs.

VISUALISE the Vortex descending into the middle of the group. You will probably sense, at this time, many other beings around our Twelve. I always acknowledge this but I do not engage with them. They are there to help, protect and work with the Vortex. Also, and this has happen on every single occasion we did this physically, a Great Deva attended at the mouth of the Vortex, again I urge to recognise and appreciate this presence is one thing but to invite for a coffee is quite another. Please do not engage but a silent 'thank you' is enough as we have work to do.

VISUALISE as you repeat The Great Invocation Light, Love and Power descending through the Vortex, down into the middle of the Twelve and out into The Grid.

FIFTH STAGE

After approximately ten to fifteen minutes visualise the Light dissipating and lessening and your Triangle slowly and purposefully 'lifting' off the other Nine coworkers (the three other Triangles) until about 3 feet (1 meter) and dissolving beautifully, quietly and peacefully into the ether.

SIXTH STAGE

It is ultimately important to 'live' this process and keep focused on the reality of what we are undertaking together.

WE ASK: give this small amount of time to work with other coworkers of like spirit and motivation. Remember:

1. INTENT
2. FOCUS
3. DELIVER

LOVE, Light and Power will be our watchwords and our guide rope as we traverse the rocky way.

THE INITIATE TOLD us of the Three Stages in the Twelves work (Preparatory, Implementory and Revelatory) and the first stage we completed over a 20 year period. We are now in the Implementory stage and you have been Called.

2025 BECKONS and we must advance group work NOW. After 2025 a new teaching will emerge as the third part of the Ancient Wisdom outlined by HPB and AAB. This is not our task, we are to advance and experiment with group synthesis and group action, we, a band of brothers and sisters. Let's get to it.

OM OM OM

* * *

THE PROTOCOL WAS the most complex I had ever seen. I found it a little daunting. What held me was the notion of dissipating thoughtforms. The idea that energy could be funnelled into the hearts and minds of humanity in order to affect real change, by helping to dissipate outmoded ideas held much appeal.

I also found the following simple summary of that early Twelve protocol helpful when performing the ritual. All the elements and the procedure needed to be rehearsed and memorised, although no one in the group came out and said this. It was and still is assumed that those participating know and take full responsibility for their own full participation.

KEYWORDS for the
Working Twelve Formation

Stillness
TGI
Linking
Visualise T
Step Forward
TGI
Visualize T
Synergy
Vortex
Deva / Angel
TMU / TDI

Downpour
Distribution
Dissipation of TF
Building
Withdraw
TGI
Close

- TGI = The Great Invocation
- TDI = The Disciples Invocation (given specifically for Twelves work)
- TMU = The Mantram of Unification
- TF = Thoughtform

SEQUENCE: Link : Visualize : Downpour : Distribute : Dissipation of TF : Build : Withdraw

* * *

THE FIRST GROUP of Distant Twelves followed the protocol at the Full Moon. This decision to draw on a moment of energetic opportunity caused some difficulty for those already practicing Full Moon meditations individually or in other groups. There was a lot to adjust to. I wasn't the only one in those early days who struggled to adapt to the commitment. Yet there was something binding about the group, an energy often stimulated by aspirational messages and quotes of wisdom and feedback on experiences which all promoted a sense of group cohesion and purpose.

Something else I found helpful was a document Steven

produced on the concept of 'as if'. This concept helps me whenever I waver, just as Pascal's Wager is my way of accommodating the core tenets of Twelves.

Brother Djwhal Khul on 'as if'
(use of the creative imagination/visualization)

'You must do this through the power of the creative imagination; you must act '**as if**'; you must see this energy pouring in, literally'

'The revelation is given to the initiate *as if* there was nothing in all the world but himself (a point of tension) and a vortex of force which takes form before his eyes, revealing to him an inevitable but future activity.'

'That the capacity, innate in that imaginative creature, man, to act '*as if*', holds the solution to the problem. By the use of the creative imagination, the bridge between the lower aspect and higher can be built and constructed.

'As a man thinketh, hopeth and willeth' so is he. This is a statement of an immutable fact.'

'I would ask all to think imaginatively and to act *as if* they were accepted disciples or at least on the periphery of some ashram'

'Some time ago I told the group that initiation was simplification. Therefore, simplify your remaining years by ever acting *'as if'.*

'Then, *as if* you were consciously standing before your Master and definitely aware of my presence, dedicate yourself to the service of the Ashram for this life and the next.'

* * *

'As if' gives me the freedom to doubt and still act. It's a vital part of my commitment to non-adherence to any doctrine or creed, because it allows me to participate based on my own inner resonance with and magnetic attraction to Twelves.

As THE MONTHS WENT BY, a New Moon meditation was also added to the monthly schedule. The group grew, and Twelves formed its first group of twelve participants out of the membership pool, with another close behind. Before long, so committed were members of the group that a Permanent Twelve was formed, each member committing to remaining in that formation for a minimum of a year.

In this period, Steven asked me to help set up a Twelves website. This I did with physicist and theosophist

Murray Stentiford. I felt a heavy weight of responsibility coming up with content as this was the public face of Twelves and I didn't want to get it wrong. Thankfully, Murray offered guidance and support and helped capture the right tone. But we were both feeling uncertain as Twelves back then was very much still in genesis. Things were evolving constantly. There wasn't a great deal on the website back then as a result, and I struggled with what else to include. But at least it was there, a presence on the world wide web, which added gravitas to Twelves.

Friend of renowned Theosophist Geoffrey Hodson, Murray exemplifies the views of those wholeheartedly embracing the vision of Twelves:

> Twelves is a process that gripped me from the start, as a powerful yet relatively simple way to bring large currents of healing and redeeming Light into the non-physical energy fields of the Earth. It gives me joy to devote time and energy to such work in a regular and disciplined way.
>
> The three kinds of meditations – Triangles, TAMs and Twelves – address the need and plight of people sunk in slavery, as it often is, to their feelings and passions, in a subjective yet intensely real way. They help the Light of Spirit to leaven the noosphere of the Earth towards a realisation of a global consciousness that could enable us to live in harmony each other and with Nature.
>
> This possibility, widely held in 'spiritual' and New Age circles, is not just a pleasant belief. It has tangible support from the Tran-

scendental Meditation experiments with group work in the 1990s, which produced marked reductions in the level of violent crime and other problems in several large cities. Growing support is also coming from Lynne McTaggart's worldwide Intention work and, in a different way, Dr Joe Dispenza's striking results.

There is nothing as powerful as a coherent, focused group working from a position of purity of intent.

I see us, as dedicated workers in the physical body, holding different positions on a spectrum of consciousness from humanity to Adeptship; as vital intermediaries in a mighty flow of energy. We are links in the chain, bringing it down from the immense heights of the Masters and beyond, to a 'frequency' level more accessible to humanity.

So, what do these group meditations mean to me? I love working with kindred souls to help bring transforming Light and Power into a world that is in urgent need of it. The method must be efficient and effective, and I see Twelves as being just that.

Murray, New Zealand (this piece originally appeared on the Twelves website and is quoted in full with the author's permission)

UNLIKE MURRAY, who has remained a steady and stable force in the group, my experience in Twelves did not go smoothly. I struggled with the daily Triangles meditations. I skipped the TAMs. I felt like a fraud and an imposter.

And my commitment kept waning. Back then, Twelves was yet to really take off. Expansion was steady but slow. I valued Twelves highly as an authentic form of esoteric practice coming out of the theosophical stream, and a real advancement of Djwhal Khul's Discipleship in the New Age or DINA experiments back in the 1930s and 40s. But those DINA groups disbanded. Would the same happen to Twelves?

Despite all of my misgivings, I remained in Twelves for eighteen months. During that time, my personal life was catapulted into chaos. I moved house twice. I almost relocated from Australia to Spain. I watched in horror as bushfires razed my old home town, tearing through my parent's former farm. In amongst the domestic upheavals, I also researched and wrote the Alice Bailey biography.

In mid-2020, just as the first Permanent Twelve was created, I left. Twelves was just one more thing to deal with in what was an overloaded, confusing and stressful time. It felt like the right thing to do.

---

1. an amorphous bridging group between humanity and the hierarchy comprising individuals responsive to their own souls and oriented towards service, and collectively carrying the seeds of the new age

FINDING TWELVES: TWELVES PARTICIPANTS

*A*fter I left Twelves, I wondered if I would return. Months passed. Months of chaos and confusion in my personal life. A sense of duty kept tugging at me, insistent, pulling me back. Eventually, I took heed, and to my surprise, in the year of my absence, Twelves had flourished. Returning was disorienting as there was so much going on, but I soon found my way. I was immediately confronted with the powerful energy of the group that had developed without me. This connectedness is summed up perfectly in the words of Patrick Chouinard:

> I had that sense with Steven C. and a few others I have come into contact with through the Blavatsky, Bailey, Roerich Facebook group, and Twelves, that co-workers or group soul members are finding each other and linking up through the internet, as with Twelves.
>
> The extent of these physical plane connections between disciples is unprecedented. The

internet is a concrete externalisation or symbol of the subjective interconnections or network. We are already connected as souls, now we are connecting on mental and emotional levels through the internet and this must now be brought down to the etheric level – to light up the grid. That is what Twelves is about. The Hierarchy cannot come among us unless the quality or vibration of humanity is raised.

WHEN I RE-ENTERED Twelves I met Vita de Waal, someone who had long intrigued me ever since I came across her name when researching Alice Bailey. Steven had told me the expansion of Twelves had much to do with her efforts. My interest in Vita was a catalyst for this book. I had it in mind to interview her, showcase her somehow, give voice to her story as someone who has drawn much inspiration from the Bailey books and applied it in her work life. She responded wholeheartedly. Seeing what she had written and realising the value in portraying members' personal spiritual journeys which led them to Twelves, I then threw the door wide open and invited the whole membership to participate in the creation of this book by responding to four simple questions. Twenty-four responded, some giving a detailed account of their spiritual journey and experiences, others keeping things short.

The following contributions are thoughtful, honest and engaging. With the exception of Vita de Waal and Patrick Chouinard, only initials are used. I've written a brief intro-duction to each for the sake of flow. I begin with Vita, who joined the original Twelves in the 1980s and then joined the current incarnation. Vita is a powerhouse, a natural organiser, she has a knack for bringing people together.

She's a highly respected Twelves participant. She's also a good storyteller.

Vita (Italy)

'It started before I even knew it had started...'

It was summer and we had been at my husband's family's medieval villa in the hills of Florence. That night I was awoken by L (my husband) who pointed in front of him.

'Do you see him?' he asked, looking at me.

I could see nothing.

He then continued. 'There, in that long black tunic, with the hood.'

I still could not see anything although I was aware that my husband was convinced that he would die young. As if he read my thoughts, he continued with, 'Do you think he has come for me?'

That night we did not sleep and talked the night away.

The following day, after a pleasant evening we went to bed, only to be woken up again when L called to me saying, 'he's there...Again.'

Again, we talked the hours away, while the hooded figure stayed in the room. By then L was convinced his hour had come and that if he would fall asleep, he would not wake up. Panic had set in.

One of us then remembered that a week before, a psychologist friend had mentioned that he had been to a lecture by somebody who had mentioned discarnate beings and beings on other dimensions, and we decided to try to get his phone number. This we got in the evening, and we begged him to come over as it was difficult to imagine a third sleepless night.

He replied that there was no need to be afraid and that this strange figure appearing in the night was not Father Death. He told us to have a good night's sleep and that he would come over at ten the next morning. Relieved, we went to bed. We were exhausted as by now we had not slept for two nights. But it was not to be as the dark figure was still there, waiting. By now L was convinced that if he slept, he would not wake up, that the third night could be fatal. We chatted and chatted. I must have fallen asleep as I woke up around nine the next morning. Next to me, my husband was still breathing!

At precisely ten o'clock the bell rang and Mr X came in. He looked like any professional and it was difficult to imagine he could lecture on other dimensions or things spiritual. As L was still in the bedroom, Mr X asked me to recount what had happened. I explained and just when I had come to the end, my husband walked in, hair dishevelled, in his bathrobe. Mr X then asked him some questions, more specific questions as it was my husband who had observed this strange figure. Mr X then proceeded to explain that this presence did not mean evil, but rather this person had something to say and had chosen my husband to say it to. Mr X then told L to 'call' this person.

Surprised, L called and to his utter amazement, this hooded figure came into the lounge and Mr X asked how he could be helped. After a period spent ascertaining what the figure wanted, we came to understand he was a monk with a set of recriminations concerning his friend. Then another figure entered the room, the monk's friend, a bishop this time, with his own set of recriminations. It was a dispute needing a resolution.

L was asked to go back to the villa as a chalice was buried there that needed to be retrieved. An appointment was set for two in the afternoon a few days later. At the appointed time Mr X was there but he had also brought a young man. I personally was quite annoyed as this was such a private matter. Mr X must have read my thoughts, or my face showed this, as he said, 'he will be needed.'

A room was chosen at the villa and the two beings were invited in. There followed more explanations and recriminations between the monk and the bishop. They then told us to go and find the chalice. It was near a specific tree and we had to dig. To our utter surprise a golden medieval chalice with precious stones was found. We were first told it had to be destroyed. However, later 'they' decided that L should have it. That afternoon, those two earth-bound beings were 'released' and we returned home with the chalice and to a good night's sleep!

Before we went to bed L told me that he had also seen a German soldier in the cellar on his motorbike! In fact, the villa was requisitioned by the Germans during the war. I asked L if he wanted to help him as well, but he was not interested. Presumably, the soldier is still there. While not interested in spirituality at all, L has on other occasions had other such encounters.

This little story is a preamble to how I got to become acquainted with the teachings of DK. Fast forward a few years and I was separated from L and wondering what to do next. I was twenty-eight years old, and by then I was reading philosophers, Jung, other authors and was fired up by the deeper and more subtler aspects of life. I decided to reconnect with Mr X. We chatted and I told him that I felt very attracted by things Tibetan but was not clear on Tibetan Buddhism as the lamas I had met did not speak English. (Few did at the time.) I was starting to wonder if I should learn Tibetan or Sanskrit. He replied that the Tibetan I was looking for already had books in Italian, and he mentioned the Tibetan and Alice Bailey.

My marriage had fallen apart. It was a traumatic period though there was also this feeling that we had done what we were meant to do together. Today I understand that we had karma and it had worked out but such a time-frame does not fit the intention of marriage, to be together for life. The two realities seemingly do not fit.

I then moved city and for the next years I immersed myself in the Bailey books along with other spiritual readings including alchemy, and Manly Hall, and I became a student of Alice Bailey's Arcane School and the Rosicrucian order of AMORC.

I read for about six hours a day back then. I devoured the books. I was thirsty. Today I ask myself how this was possible, as now I can digest only a bit at a time, there are so many layers of meaning. Back then it was all so logical and natural. Parts were new but others parts were 'of course, yes, yes'.

It strikes me that encountering any teachings might be part of a path that has been traced long before that. That there is a timing. A bit like when you are ready the Teacher appears.

I remember entering St Peters in Rome when I was three, and going with our indigenous Quetchua cook to ceremonies when I was five or six, and knowing things in the Bible, like the name of cities or the names of the brothers of Joseph. I remember at the age of ten crying about Christ being crucified and that I did not want this to happen again. There clearly was a continuum in this sense.

After my separation from L, when I had started my reading period and was yet to start on DK, I had this experience of non-duality and realised we are all part of God, in differing degrees of awareness. That in this sense we were all Sons of The One, Christs in the Making. I remember thinking, 'I cannot tell anybody, as they will think me blasphemous, crazy'. Only after many years of

Tibetan Buddhist mahamudra and dzogchen meditation practice have I come to realise that this is the natural state, this non-dual realisation, only that it requires stabilising, through daily practice; something I don't do often enough. That is why retreats are important as they provide the space and time to foster the stabilisation of the non-dual realisation as a natural state, that part each of us has but gives no attention to or thinks it only manifests in 'special people'. No! This is who we really are! Beyond the conditioning of separation and 'the other'.

Reading spiritual teachings for six hours a day felt exhilarating. It was a journey of discovery and at the same time a confirmation of what I sensed before, what I 'knew' without knowing. I was aware it was the first time I had read it but somehow what was written was 'familiar'.

I then started reading loads of different things, and one day I got a bit of automatic writing, a clear message that I heed to this day: that not all of the texts I was reading were okay, that black will portray itself as white, that I needed to discriminate when it came to what I took in.

In 2000 I had my second and so far, my last piece of automatic writing.

I think the years between twenty-eight and thirty-five are when you start gaining a direction in your life. It became clear that spirituality was going to be part of my life, in one way or the other. I allow myself to go on intuition and as such I am not stuck and will always see if the spiritual can be integrated in everyday life. I am aware that there is a universal approach. Being multicultural and having been exposed to many types of beliefs, I need to be able to render a teaching into everyday language, devoid of jargon, which is not easy. Any teaching is but a step towards full integration, when self recognises Self and the search is over and teachings are not needed anymore. We then discover that what we searched for all our life has all along been there!

I don't think glamour has had much impact on me because I respect many teachings and see many having a role. A teaching can be separative if used in isolation, while my instinct is to bring people together. I remember at a Lucis Trust conference the Italians sitting without really speaking together – to me that was an opportunity wasted. I herded them together and we created World Goodwill Italy and were then given the publishing arm of the Bailey books and met up in Italy. I met up with Mary Bailey and coordinated part of her trip when she came to Italy as by then there was a group to receive her.

Back then, I never planned to do anything with all that spiritual knowledge, as I was aware of the layers of meaning and that so much more would still be learned. Also, that different teachings would appeal to different people and mindsets, and as such one teaching was not necessarily more or better. What I liked about DK was the amazing array of areas, his language. It became clear from the start that one lifetime would not be enough to learn from those teachings. Very humbling. And I am no intellectual so I knew my limits from the start. Plus, I am not disciplined. I am tenacious, though. I am 'elastic' if one can apply this word to spirituality.

When I decided I wanted to give much more time to the spiritual part in my life I went on a journey of discovery, exploring various Theosophists, Anthroposophy, and Alice Bailey, and I settled on DK. I was soon asked to join the Lucis Trust in Geneva. Yet I was also attracted to Findhorn, where all these traditions come together. At Findhorn, people can practice their chosen tradition, there was that freedom and respect.

Around 1974 I met Ezio Savoini at the Lucis Conference in Geneva. We became friends, corresponded, and I visited him on various occasions, chatting for hours on end. It was Ezio who had translated many of the Bailey books into Italian and it was he who translated and brought Agni Yoga to Italy. He had a deep knowledge of the ageless wisdom teachings, of harmonics and the lambdoma. He shared with me the concept along ray sequence of the six-pointed star. He made it clear that this was one way to work but that there might be other ways.

I thought of Ezio and his six-pointed star when I joined the original Twelves group in the 1980s as Twelves are two six-pointed stars along the same ray sequence Ezio recognised a decade earlier. After I met and worked with Robert, Peter and Steven, I was amazed at how diverse they were and as such how complementary.

Last October (2020) I rejoined Twelves, which was unexpected. I am seventy-five years old now and looking back I can see a logical sequence. However, at each crossroad in my life, I have often been in doubt as to what road to take. Today I see that each segment had to happen in order to get to the next one. Twelves has shown me this in such a way as to be 'without doubt'.

We thought Twelves in 2001 was the end. For the two or three years before I re-joined Twelves, I felt that I needed to create space for something else and started training a person to step into my space at the United Nations where I networked with NGOs, organised events, and saw opportunities for cooperation. At the United Nations I felt that my role was to be a bridge builder. As far as I knew, Twelves was finished and did not exist so I was curious about what would 'appear'. The last thing I imagined was to hear from Steven. I had looked for him, out of curiosity, and I even thought he might have died.

Then everything slotted in, almost against my will, as it all went so quickly. I still had a crucial text for Twelves work, and at the time, even Steven couldn't find his copy, which showed me that I was meant to be back in this. I took up my 'part' in an organic way, not stepping on anybody's toes.

* * *

VITA'S spiritual awareness opened through a direct engagement with the spirit world, and, like me, a direct introduction to the Bailey books. An intensely spiritual woman with eclectic interests, Vita has avoided the sectarian trap. This same eclecticism can be found in the testimonies of others.

RH (Mexico)

The Path of the Seeker

'I will go through this life only once, and any act of good or kindness I have to do now, because I will not return.'

MY SEARCH BEGAN when some friends invited my husband and I to take a course in metaphysics. There I began to hear for the first time about the existence of the ascended Masters, the Divine spark, meditation and other topics that throughout my life have served as a basis to start my path as a seeker of the Light.

I started at home, giving self-improvement courses to a small group of people, with the satisfaction of seeing how their lives were changing, giving meaning to their existence as well as finding a bit of peace and tranquillity. Among the topics, we taught them relaxation techniques to remove tension, which in addition to giving you a little peace, gives health to your body.

I continued for several years teaching the courses that had enriched my life and that I wanted to share with others because they made a contribution and gave spiritual support to my life and that of my family.

On this path I met Carmen Santiago from the New Thought Foundation of Venezuela, which further enriched my life, because together with her I embarked on the search for knowledge of my essence, learning the work of some Masters of the spiritual hierarchy, which has served as a model and a source of guidance in life.

As congresses and retreats are organised every year in the different foundations located in countries such as Puerto Rico, Argentina and Cuba, and cities such as Miami, I had the opportunity to meet many brothers committed to work and service, with whom we continue to meet now regularly, virtually with the work in connection with Shambala, with the formation of molecules formed by groups of twelve people. It is a monthly meditation, and we also do the work with the violet flame. These meditations are organised on Zoom to help save the planet.

Through Carmen I got to know the books of Master D.K., Madame Blavatsky, Annie Besant, the Count of Saint Germain or Racosky, in short, I got to know the work of some Masters who make up the spiritual hierarchy, including Master el Morya. I met Master Parvathi Kumar and his WT organisation, the World Teacher Trust (trust in the World Teacher).

Every month a global meditation of the violet flame is organised and one called connection with Shambala. We meet virtually, but constantly, since it has been possible to consolidate a committed group of true servers for the work of the spiritual hierarchy. We follow the Master's talks through Zoom, and Whatsapp groups have been formed with which we follow the teaching of the hierarchy through the sending of books and messages. I write all this because it is a background of my meditation work with the Twelves group.

I came across Twelves through Facebook. They said that whoever wanted to be part of a group of twelve people to work on the Full Moon and New Moon meditations should write, so I did and Vita de Waal, who is part of this organisation, answered me and sent the information by email, and with the background of the Shambhala connection work done in Carmen's group, it was easy for me to understand the purpose of the group.

* * *

SOMETIMES, those seeking an authentic spiritual life experience an awakening, an epiphany triggered by an intense experience, which can be thought of as the birth of a fresh beginning involving the revelation of meaning. Through depictions of these moments, it becomes easy to see a blending of the mystic and esoteric ways of knowing.

CL (ITALY)

I WILL HAPPILY SHARE my experience which unfortunately I have to summarise due to the complexity of the series of events. I was very young when I asked myself the reason for life and death. I asked myself many questions and I was convinced that the answers would come sooner or later. At fifteen years old, after many adventures I met an ancient herbalist, the One who later turned out to be my instructor and Brother on the Way. There was an immediate impact of awareness, even though I was very young and he was almost fifty years old.

Magic had to happen and after a few years my dream came true. My first most significant experience was on a Sunday. I had to meet with my instructor and another guy. I woke up very happy and joyful. By then I was eighteen and still not practicing meditation, but my instructor told me to raise my consciousness and recite the Great Invocation, that Sunday before leaving the house. So I did recite the GI aloud with deep aspiration and finally I came to say aloud the One I believed to be my Master.

Immediately afterwards I had a strong shiver in my upper body with a strong tingling in the centre of my head as if a small hole had opened. All of this with watery eyes and a strong dizziness in the head, but without any pain, just a feeling of peace and joy. At the time, I had no idea what had happened to me. I got up like an automaton and went to the books. I picked one at random. It was *Letters on Occult Meditation* by Alice A. Bailey. I opened a page at random, and there was the chapter that dealt with the access of the Masters and how it was permeated. On that very page there was a description of everything that had just happened to me.

For three days I was invaded by that powerful energy and vibration that was indescribable, and since then I have understood that it was the vibration of the Master. Then, after a few years I had a dream experience with two Beings I did not know who asked me if I wanted to collaborate with Them to help my fellow men. My answer was yes, with all my mind and with all my heart. I woke up with the lucid memory of the dream with every sentence said. I told it to my instructor who said, 'Now you can write and ask to be accepted in the Arcane School.' It was the begin-

ning of the year 1972. From there my great adventure
began.

At the beginning of the 1980s, I was called to collaborate in the work of the six-pointed star plus the central,
organised by a disciple from Turin. I participated with
great enthusiasm because it was Hierarchical Work. I felt
the same enthusiasm when I joined Twelves. I believe that
the two groups were born at the same time and the two
complete each other. I am proud to be part of Twelves.

* * *

MANY IN TWELVES lead rich spiritual lives, lives of
dedication and commitment to furthering the teachings
that have inspired them in the course of their lives. The
spiritual life is the life of service and time and again in
Twelves, this is evident in the testimony of members.

SEO (USA)

I WENT from being an atheistic scientist, to agnostic, to
humanist, and then to the grand conflict.

The grand conflict elicited a search for that 'something
else' to which my intuition pointed. That journey led to
NLP, Ayurveda, Ecuadorian shamans, Anthroposophy,
Rosicrucianism, a Golden Dawn offshoot, Lucis Trust
Arcane School, and Twelves. I have in me a book about
the Ecuadorian shamanic experience, and perhaps also the
Golden Dawn offshoot and the many wrong turns there
(with a few critical 'right' turns as well). In addition to my
work-for-pay, I donate my abilities to bring a Waldorf-
inspired school (we are implementing a high school now!)
to my region. Waldorf/Anthroposophy practices decision-

making by consensus, which is a new concept for me, and a difficult structure under which to operate. I am learning a lot!

Rudolf Steiner/Anthroposophy led to Madame Blavatsky/Theosophy, then to the Alice Bailey/DK Teachings. The DK teachings settled in my soul with an intuitional alignment and feeling of homecoming. They help to fuse the elements of every other spiritual teaching in my experience together, and serve as a guide to my life impulse and way of being.

I had long sought a form of service that could contribute to the well-being of the world at an energetic level. Twelves is not tainted by money for services, or individual power or authority. Twelves feels to me like a pure path of service, and one that does not preclude the practice of any other service.

Here's an elucidation of my current work and AAB/DK/Twelves influence. I am involved in a grassroots re-founding of a school that is dedicated to the renewal of education. The school, rising like a Phoenix from the ashes of an ill-advised merger, emerged with an impulse for reinvention and was founded on the principles of living thinking. It draws from the original intentions of Rudolf Steiner's educational work and tries to further develop those ideas through an experiential understanding of how human consciousness unfolds. Rather than focusing on content of classes, the fundamental ground of the school's programs is a conscious understanding of how human beings develop. We seek to develop a keen perceptive capacity and awareness in each individual, to find new patterns and relationships through living thinking, and elicit an interest and enthusiasm to take these abilities and initiate changes in one's own life and the culture around us. My contributions to the school are inspired by AB and DK, and supported and furthered by my Twelves practice.

'The true education is consequently the science of linking up the integral parts of man, and also of linking him up in turn with his immediate environment, and then with the greater whole in which he has to play his part.' Alice Bailey, *Education in the New Age*

* * *

THERE ARE many pathways a seeker may walk down on their journey of spiritual awakening and growth. The traditional practices of folk spiritualities attract many and it is through those practices that seekers are drawn more deeply into the esoteric.

CS (Philippines)

MY SPIRITUAL JOURNEY began during my teenage years. However, during this time I was more interested in Wicca and Shamanism. I enjoyed the earth-centred spirituality that these paths represented for me. My interest in Wicca and Shamanism led me to join various spiritual and occult organisations. This included Buddhist groups, shamanic groups, Rosicrucian groups, etc. It also led me to the Theosophical Society.

I became a member of the Theosophical Society around 2004. I enjoyed the intellectual freedom within the society – there is no dogma, no enforced beliefs, just exploring the different spiritual ideas and concepts. I also enjoyed the paradigm or the spiritual map of reality that Theosophy provided me. One of the reasons I started my spiritual journey was because of my curiosity about life. I wanted, figuratively speaking, to break life and the universe down to see how it ticks.

Theosophy and the Theosophical Society provided such an avenue for me. Theosophy gave me a worldview that could answer many questions about life. It provided me with answers but never really forced them into me. My first exposure to the Alice Bailey/DK teachings came soon after. I was still studying psychology at a famous Catholic University here in the Philippines. The University that year hosted a book fair within the campus. I was surprised that some of my Theosophical friends were manning a bookstand sponsored by the Ageless Wisdom Library. The stand only had twenty-four titles all from the same author. These, of course, were the twenty-four books of the Ageless Wisdom by Alice Bailey.

I was slowly introduced to these teachings as some of my friends and I started to volunteer in the Ageless Wisdom Library on weekends. At this point, I did not think much of the Alice Bailey teachings. I thought they were just another set of channelled materials like Jane Roberts or Edgar Cayce. I did enjoy the company of my friends though, and so I continued to volunteer during weekends.

I started to read many of the books. I found many quite interesting like *initiation, Human and Solar, A Treatise on White Magic,* and *the Soul and its Mechanism.* However, one book stood out from these and that is *Glamour: A World Problem.* After reading this book I felt I needed to re-evaluate my spiritual path. I felt that many of my experiences practicing Wicca and Shamanism were glamour.[1] I needed to check how I viewed my life as these views, too, may have been influenced by glamour.

I enrolled in Arcane School soon after, in 2008. I had just finished my degree in Nursing during this time. I was working full time in the hospital and did not have regular time to attend lodge meetings in the TS. I am happy that the Arcane School provided a new avenue for me to learn the Ageless Wisdom. Regrettably, back in those days we still sent physical letters, and the response time was not as quick as it is today using email.

I enjoyed studying at the Arcane School. It gave me a steady curriculum I could follow. The meditations also provided me with something I could practice alongside the theoretical knowledge I obtained from studying in the TS and the Arcane School.

Despite my busy schedule, I remained active in both the TS and the Arcane School. Soon both organisations had to set up their presences on social media. In line with this, I also created several FB groups for some lodges and meditation groups.

This was when I first encountered the Facebook group Blavatsky Bailey Roerich. This Facebook group was spearheaded by Steven Chernikeeff. He was trying to create a pool of students from these three great teachers. I joined this Facebook group and was very active for some time.

Eventually, Steven introduced the concept of Twelves to some members of the Blavatsky Bailey Roerich group. Twelves is essentially an expansion of the Triangles work outlined by DK in the Alice Bailey Teachings. I had good experiences previously in working with Triangles. There was a time when I was living in a place that was considered a 'rough' side of the neighbourhood. I was thinking of moving out when I started the Triangles work. It seems that after a few weeks, the area became a bit more peaceful and safer. I eventually moved out of that area as well but I remember how the atmosphere seemed to have changed after a few weeks of Triangle work.

One of the challenges of Triangles is to keep your co-workers interested in the work. I often thought about what would happen if my co-workers lost interest and I would be the only one continuing with the Triangle. I then had a dream that there were people who were 'fixing' the lines of light in the Triangle network. I reported this in one of my meditation reports in Arcane School. I received material regarding the esoteric work of Triangles. This is a more advanced form of Triangles that does seem to work in 'fixing' the lines in the worldwide Triangle network.

Eventually, my fellow Triangle workers did lose interest. Luckily at this time, the Twelves network was being formed. As part of the Twelves network, we also did the regular daily Triangles work.

* * *

FINDING TWELVES via the Triangles network is a common point of entry into Twelves. For Twelves, this has the advantage of building a membership out of those already experienced in the technique. Most in Twelves are familiar with Alice Bailey and have studied the books, got involved with Triangles or undertaken esoteric training in the Arcane School.

TS (Slovenia)

A FRIEND, spiritual counsellor, and co-traveller on the spiritual path Aristid Havliček – Tili – brought me into contact with the Twelves initiative in the fall of 2019. We are a group from Slovenia, and we have been gathering regularly twice a week for more than three decades. In our early days – the late 80s – some met Robert Adams and Peter Maslin of the original Twelves group during their visit to London and New York. I met them both during a visit to Slovenia in 1986.

We were also aware of the third member of this initiative – Steven. It was a time of the intensive building of the Triangles grid all over the world.

During the last thirty years or so, the situation of our world has deteriorated immensely. After reading *Esoteric Apprentice* and *2025*, it was an easy choice to answer the call to join Twelves, because there were no other choices. A lot is at stake for humanity and Gaia – our generous host. So, one after another, all members of our group joined!

* * *

OFTEN, seeking begins through healing, either seeking healing for oneself or to help others.

DI (USA)

I GREW up in an atheist but really spiritual family. As they raised us, my parents taught us to follow the golden rule, that the boomerang will always come back and to always be mindful of that, that the world is run by laws of Mother Nature.

In 2018 I was steered towards pranic healing and it changed my life and the life of my family completely. Through it, I was introduced to the teachings of Master DK and the Ancient Wisdom. I firmly believe that I had to deserve it, that there was karma to be worked out on my part before I was given the wonderful gift of pranic healing and arhatic yoga.

Around the time of Wesak 2020, I found out about the plans for the reappearance of the World Teacher and that became my obsession, and I was praying for the way to help the process.

I believe that my knowledge and understanding of the

matter had to reach a certain point when I could become of service, and at that point through synchronicities I was led to Twelves.

In June 2021, as always, and particularly during the Christ festival and the summer solstice, I was obsessed with the Reappearance of Christ and the Hierarchy, praying and asking how I could be of help in the process. This time I started hearing this voice in my head. It was very clear. I had heard it in the past and I had always thought these were my own thoughts. This time, the voice was telling me to join Facebook again. I started having a debate with the voice: 'No, I do not want to go back to Facebook, it censors, does psychological experiments with the unsuspecting users'. The voice did not give up, telling me, 'If you join, you can join the Alice Bailey, Master DK Daily Quote group which you enjoyed so much' (and I did miss it a lot). After a few days, I finally conceded and agreed to download Facebook again to my phone. Within a day or two of me doing so, there was a post in the Reappearance of Christ Alice Bailey daily page, and at the bottom of it, there was an invitation to serve and the link to the Twelves website.

I was immediately drawn to it. While perusing the website, I ordered the *Esoteric Apprentice* the very same day. Reading through the website and The Initiate's *Discourses*, even before finishing this book, I signed up to join Twelves. I was very excited, taking notes, digesting the book slowly, mostly in the wee hours of the morning. The voice reappeared, now repeating that I was a sleeper, that I had incarnated to do this work. Silly parallels of the Manchurian Candidate came to my mind, and I was having fun with it, until one early morning I came to the part of the book where the Sleepers were mentioned. This struck me to my core, I was quite in a state of a shock. The experience gave a whole new meaning to the voice I always thought was 'just my thoughts'.

* * *

A CONTINUING THEME, a thread running through these accounts of the spiritual life, is a heartfelt philosophical probing, a yearning for meaning and significance. Among Twelves members, this journey often leads to the Arcane School.

PATRICK CHOUINARD (CANADA)

I CAME into the Bailey teachings at a young age. At the age of 16 I was introduced to Buddhism by my father's temporary secretary (I worked on weekends at his company). It was just the two of us. She spoke about karma and reincarnation. I was enthralled. Suddenly life had purpose and I had a thirst to learn more.

The same woman gave me a book on meditation. I brought it with me to class. A fellow student noticed it and invited me to Bev's place. She told me it was an informal place where they did weekly group meditations and often hung out on other days, discussing spiritual matters, drawing, playing guitar, etc. I was intrigued and anxious to meet fellow seekers.

Beverly Golby was a wonderful forty-six-year-old single mother who opened her home to a bunch of young people from the suburbs. She was a dedicated seeker of truth and very into Alice Bailey (DK) along with Vera Stanley Alder, Douglas Baker, White Eagle, Ram Dass and others (all of whose books were available to us all). Though not a scholarly type she was very insightful. She was intuitive, musical, and very into astrology. Her favourite book was Bailey's *The Labours of Hercules* depicting twelve tests or spiritual lessons each relating to a sign of the zodiac.

It was there that I was introduced to astrology. It was to become one of my great loves. We all knew each other's signs and I began to see specific traits in action and could feel the energy of their signs. Very distinct. In time I could often guess someone's sign after a few minutes with them (particularly Aries, Leo and Taurus - whose features often do resemble the animal representing the sign).

Astrology has been proven in my experience, and particularity after studying my chart and those of others.

I read Dane Rudhyar's *Astrology of Personality* around that time. He opened up new vistas, giving a deeper understanding of astrology. He had quite an impact on me. His book Beyond Individualism impacted me greatly with the ideas of trans-cultural or planetary consciousness and of seed men and women.

Later I delved into DK's *Esoteric Astrology* and I have been studying it ever since. It's no coincidence that most of my closest friends in the DK community are also astrologers, though it was not like we initially connected or became friends based on that common interest. It just happened that way – that I just felt a special connection to them – though I don't think our friendship is coincidental.

Noticing this played a role in my deeper commitment to esoteric astrology as a form of service – a soul purpose. I have also befriended a couple of astrologers not into DK, and whom I met by chance.

Not surprisingly the first book I read from DK was *A Treatise on White Magic*. Besides years of studying DK and of meditation, and related things (being faculty at the Morya Federation and teaching in the Theosophical Society, both which included group meditation), I have a particular interest in the kind of white magic group work Twelves is doing. My attraction to it that began soon after I discovered DK when I became part of a small esoteric group in the 80s that used advanced group meditations for service with a particular focus on colour and sound (we called ourselves the Aquarian World Servers and our vision was to establish an intentional community to implement some of DK's ideas).

I was always drawn to that magical aspect of DK, along with esoteric astrology, his teachings on initiation, and the wisdom component in DK's work – notably to be found in the Discipleship books and elsewhere where he deals with challenges facing disciples.

Early on I was drawn in particular to *Letters on Occult Meditation* (naturally his chapters on colour and sound) and *A Treatise on White Magic*. His pages on the collective use of form in LOM struck me as very important. There he talks about how groups can contact and be conduits for the energies of higher Beings (for example the Spirit of Peace) through the creation of a funnel. Using sound for the benefit of humanity struck me as being key; the OM primarily, and invocations, sounded in the right way with love and faith or positive expectancy.

DK says that the just as forces of evil tap into or invoke the energies of cosmic evil that way, so can we invoke the forces of Light on behalf of humanity. And that the door to those forces of Light will be opened for humanity by groups of disciples by a united use of spiritual will expressed in SOUND.

Years ago, I read *The Way to Shambhala* by Edwin Bernbaum in which he recounts the prophecy of the coming King of Shambhala, who along with his army of warriors, will overthrow the forces of evil. Interestingly he writes that they will do this through the power of sound (mantrashakti). This has been a focus I have had in DK's work – the science of invocation and evocation, and the urgency for small groups to use the Great Invocation (including the 2nd Stanza given in 1940) with more power. Especially now given the world situation and during this special cycle of spiritual opportunity (1965-2025) where our potential for impact is great. That is what Twelves is doing.

I read the book Agni Yoga around the same time I read the Shambhala book. I was particularly struck by his statement about the potential power of small groups, especially a group of twelve.

The 1980s was the first phase of DK students coming together. The second being in recent years through the internet which has brought so many of us together, primarily through Facebook. I have befriended dozens of very serious students of DK through Facebook. I joined the Blavatsky, Bailey and Roerich Facebook group nearly a decade ago and have shared extensively in it. It is through BBR that I fortunately made the connection with Steven Chernikeeff, who started it.

One of the things that I appreciate about Steven's narrative in his Twelves book *Esoteric Apprentice* is the humility that comes through:

> For anyone to say, 'I would change nothing' sounds arrogant to me. When I reflect on my life there are many things I would improve, things I would not say and kindnesses I would render more unequivocally. In my group work the same applies. *Esoteric Apprentice*, p.92 1st ed.

THERE IS no grandiose claim-making about himself in his book, and he is self-effacing and transparent. Totally unglamorous. And so what if he receives instructions from an initiate? In this the most critical phase of humanity's entire evolution, this imminent birth of the Christ within humanity – taking the first initiation en masse involving a great spiritual awakening – along with the externalisation of the Hierarchy including all the disruption that involves, not to mention the forces at work trying to thwart both eventualities; do we really think there would be no communication between the Hierarchy and humanity besides the blue books? Of course there are disciples and initiates receiving new instructions, impressions or guidance to deal with whatever challenges come along, and to implement some of the possibilities mentioned by DK. Steven Chernikeeff is one of them.

* * *

THIS DEEP CONNECTION with the Alice Bailey/DK teachings is evident in the following contribution, which serves to reveal the many and varied ways DK students become involved in this form of esoteric knowledge and practice, involvement that leads to Twelves.

TH (DENMARK)

THE DK TEACHINGS HAVE, since the early twenties, been central to my spiritual developmental process. And after the Harmonic Convergence 1987 they became my primary

Inspiration source alongside The Teachings of The Danish incarnate Initiate Jes Bertelsen.

My spiritual history includes involvement in the Rosegarden Spiritual Center, Copenhagen (World Healing Services), Antahkarana School for Esoteric Healing & Illumination Therapy, the Arcane School, the Lucis Trust's Full Moon Meditations and World Goodwill. I'm a constituting member of the Danish Interfaith Forum and the Djwhal Khul College, Esoteric School. I helped initiate the NIPS/Nordic Information Centre for the Institute for Planetary Synthesis. And I gained a Masters Degree in Esoteric Psychology at the University of The Seven Rays and joined their PhD.E. Programme in Esoteric Psychological Philosophy. I'm now part of the Golden Circle Denmark Esoteric Teachings and Full Moon Meditation Services. I joined Twelves in order to offer my skills for this above Divine assistance task.

* * *

MANY WHO FIND inspiration in the Bailey teachings have come from a Christian background. Some, like Alice Bailey herself, rejecting the faith instilled in them as a child in favour of Theosophy. There is much in the teachings that would resonate with those brought up with Christianity, especially Alice Bailey's use of the key turning points in the life of Jesus as examples of the main initiations of the spiritual path. The switch from religious belief to esoteric practice is as much about the style of engagement as it is an embracing of the world of meaning that esoteric knowledge provides. The following contribution captures the sense of belonging many find in Twelves.

SH (AUSTRALIA)

. . .

BY THE TIME I came to Twelves, I was a long-time meditator and student of DK teachings. Ever a seeker, in my childhood I was drawn to organised religion (packed off to Sunday school to give the parents peace!), and I enjoyed the beauty and energy of ancient churches and the hymns (not so much the sermons and some of the prayers and readings). But there was definitely something missing. I flirted very briefly with Catholicism because I liked the idea of confession and forgiveness and was somewhat envious of those who seemed so satisfied and secure in their belief system. But it didn't satisfy me, there were so many unanswered questions, I wanted more!

Discovering meditation in my thirties was a Godsend. This was more like it! I practiced diligently, peeling away the layers, devouring information and books and joining every workshop and course that came along. Over the years, I studied much of DKs teachings, participated in world service mediations and worked with small groups of students, sharing and teaching in practical ways. As we moved on from snail mail to instant communication, I found Triangles online and there connected with JGG and ultimately Twelves.

* * *

THERE'S OFTEN a latent or active mystical way of knowing evident in those arriving at DK and then eventually Twelves. This way of knowing transmutes or fuses with an esoteric way of knowing. The result is a spiritual awareness perfectly suited to Twelves work.

JGG (USA)

. . .

I GREW up attending the Episcopal Church in my small hometown with my mother and four siblings. My father was a lapsed Catholic and got to sleep in. I was very attentive in church and resonated deeply with the teachings of Love and Charity given by Jesus Christ, as interpreted in the Gospels and lessons that were read by the minister and various male parishioners. I was very empathic with those around me, though I didn't know what to do with those feelings. I remember holding my own services in my bedroom with shades drawn, clothing over lamps to deepen the shadows and provide a sacred atmosphere as I knelt by my bed to pray. I imagined becoming a nun, though I had no idea what that meant and the only nuns I had ever seen or heard of were the mean ones at the local Catholic school that my friends told me about. (I went to a public school.) Or the flying nun on TV.

Interactions with and observations of adults served to confuse me regarding Jesus' message, or at least how society interpreted and applied it. When I tried to articulate my view of how the world should be, based on my understanding of Christian principles, my father declared, 'You're a communist!' I had no idea what that meant but could tell it was something anathema to my father. I witnessed my mother wondering aloud what she would do if there was a black person next to her at the communion rail and she had to drink from the communion cup after them. Then there was the neighbour from across the street who so piously and self-righteously read the Sunday lesson and later could be heard screaming at his wife and daughter.

As time went on, I grew disillusioned, while still attending church to please my mother as outward rebellion wasn't my style. I had learned to keep my thoughts to myself. Although I usually went with a hangover following some heavy partying and dancing at a local bar on Saturday night into Sunday morning.

In contrast to the traditional religious upbringing, I came across books about reincarnation, UFOs, Atlantis, The Lost Continent of Mu, and Edgar Cayce. I read these books voraciously but never discussed them with anyone that I recall. They opened my mind to other ideas and realities beyond the mundane, concrete world.

My choice to attend college and my path after entering are also part of my spiritual unfoldment, although I didn't realise it until later. I was determined to get out of my small town, feeling the certainty that if I stayed there I would languish and be relegated to working as a salesgirl in the local dime store. I had had a number of painful and confusing experiences growing up and contention with my father, that was more internal than external, as I didn't have insight and I didn't know how to express myself. I was shy and depressed, which I compensated for with partying and sneaky rebellions. My mother somehow empathised, or was influenced from Spirit, and made sure that I was able to leave home and go to school.

With a combination of small loans and scholarships, I enrolled in a state college about an hour from home. I wanted to get away but couldn't completely break. I had determined that I wanted to be a Medical Technologist as I enjoyed Science, especially Biology, and I loved looking into a microscope. But Spirit had other plans for me. I struggled with college chemistry, and after three semesters of Cs and Ds, I decided to throw in the towel. I spent several weeks agonising about my next step. Another major? I considered several options, but none truly resonated. Go to California and live with my father's family for a while? I was too shy to live among virtual strangers and not so adventurous as to forge my way in a completely different part of the country. Return to my parents' house? Absolutely not!

My mother once again came to my rescue. Somehow she found out about a new major starting the next semester: Occupational Therapy. I researched it and felt drawn to the description of assisting others in a very practical way, fulfilling my impulse to help. And so I was directed from the world of interacting with things to the world of interacting with people. I have been on that Path since.

There is more to that story that I could tell as I continued to be directed to the right Path for me, meeting the right people, finding the right opportunities. I have worked as a Psychiatric Occupational Therapist for forty-three years, helping others and saving and developing myself, emotionally, mentally, and spiritually in the process. I recognise the intertwining and progression of the personal, professional, and spiritual throughout my life.

My next years were the traditional path of getting married, buying a house, having a baby, feeling settled, but everything changed around the time of my first Saturn return. I was one of the few white people working in an African American community hospital. After a period of time, the people that I worked with me accepted me and sort of raised me up into a more self-conscious adult. I'm referring to self-consciousness in terms of my personal feelings, needs, impulses, desires, thoughts and opinions. That self-consciousness took me on both a profound and a painful journey. I'll focus on the profound since it's the topic of inquiry, but I will say that the painful was the probably typical story of the Prodigal Daughter, comprised of sex, drugs, and rock and roll as I struggled with awakened self-awareness.

The nurse educator on the psychiatric unit on which I

was employed approached me and said that she taught at a school that she thought I would be interested in. I don't remember what she said, whether she gave me materials to read, or how it happened, but I enrolled in the Baltimore Spiritual Science Center and studied there for the next five years. A different kind of explosion went off emotionally, mentally, and spiritually as I read Blavatsky, Bailey, Leadbeater, Hall, and learned to meditate and work with energies, participate in Healing Services, connect with my higher self and intuition, and had various types of readings – Ray, Astrological, Intuitive.

In my second year, two sisters, Anne and Dorothy, arrived from California with a book that catapulted me into my next level of development, and this is directly related to my much later arrival at Twelves. The book is titled *The Rainbow Bridge* by Norman and Josephine Stevens. The connection with those two sisters and that book had another profound impact on my life as I learned much from them, devoured the book, practiced the techniques, participated in Full Moon meditations, and eventually travelled to Los Angeles and experienced the unique energies there. I encountered Devas, planted Buddhic columns, and finally met the venerable Norman Stevens himself. He told me I was here to take the third initiation. I filed that away in my mind, not really knowing what to do with that information, just as I hadn't known what to do with one of his daughter's comments that when she had seen me in the spiritual science class she had wondered, 'What's a Brother doing here?'

My Path diverged from the deeply esoteric after graduating from BSSC, but spirituality remained an important part of my life in varying forms, and I continued contact with Lucis Trust via their website and newsletters. I recognised my work in psychiatry as an occupational therapist and healer as being spiritual service, and that has deepened greatly over the years of my career. I've enjoyed deep friendships over decades with women I met through that work. Through them I joined a Wiccan group called Gaia's Circle in the early 90s.

Participation in Gaia's Circle rituals taught me about the rhythms of the Earth and the Seasons, their symbolic meaning, and how those cycles are mirrored within us. As above, so below. I continue to honour those rhythms. The relationships formed there are the deepest of my life. I'm still in contact with many of the women. Four are among my very best friends. We are in continual contact via a text thread and we get together in person regularly. I've had much more difficulty in integrating the spiritual into my relationships with men. That has been my greatest challenge, but seems to have been finally worked through. I'm now happily and contentedly single. I feel that is part of my Divine Plan as I have few distractions from the Work of Twelves that I have embraced.

Finding and joining Twelves directly links back to my studies at BSSC and meeting the two daughters of Norman and Josephine Stevens. I read their book *The Rainbow Bridge* and practiced the techniques there and engaged in the activities mentioned prior. After a while the activity lessened but I remained in touch via the Lucis Trust website and their newsletters. I read about Triangles with interest, and I might have signed up, but I never developed contacts or practice. I was devoted to Wicca and incorporated the understandings gleaned into my daily life.

About four years ago, in response to long term sleep problems, a friend suggested that I try the Insight Timer app. I followed through and almost immediately was invited to a Triangles Meditation Group. I was amazed at this fortuitous occurrence and readily accepted and started joining with people in Triangles right away. The administrator of this group is Starling Hunter who is known to many in the spiritual community on Facebook. He had something set up on Insight Timer so that everyone who joined was automatically offered an invitation to join Triangles.

As I joined with others in Triangles, I also networked with new people to help them understand the process and connect with others, pretty much what I do now in Twelves. Starling noticed and made me a Moderator, a role I took on with great zeal, understanding the importance, and later the urgency, of building and strengthening the Planetary Network of Light.

I found the Triangles Meditation Group on Facebook and started attending their webinars. One of the webinars mentioned the goal of 144,000 Triangles by 2025. This served to heighten my own sense of urgency and I was tireless in my work that the IT group add to the numbers. I also started feeling a longing for something, though I didn't know what. More study, another BSSC in a different format? Deeper understanding, commitment, another turn of the spiral? I wasn't sure, but I started spending more time on Facebook following people who posted on the Triangles page and seemed to have very deep and varied knowledge and understanding that I didn't have, but thought I wanted. Finally, I came across a post regarding a book called *2025 and The World Teacher*. I immediately downloaded and devoured it. At the end there were links to Twelves Facebook Group and another book, *Esoteric Apprentice*. I applied to the group and downloaded that book in the same moment.

I've doubted that I was 'good enough' or 'evolved enough', but I've never doubted that Twelves is where I'm supposed to be and this is the work that I'm meant to do.

* * *

OFTEN, the spiritual path is a series of stepping stones and turning points involving the opening of a book or an introduction to a spiritual teacher of some kind, someone further along the long and arduous journey. Those brought up in the Christian faith might find their own connection to faith and engagement with religious practice begins to open the door. There's a sense, too, in all of these contributions, that Twelves marks a significant moment, a flowering culmination of all the preceding decades of learning and practicing.

JG (USA)

IT WAS NEVER a conscious dream of mine to follow a spiritual path, but in retrospect, the path was paved perfectly. I was born in Central California (USA) and raised in a Roman Catholic family. Our practice of religion was just about routine without lesson: church on Sunday, fasting before church, and classes to receive the sacraments of communion, confession, and confirmation. My understanding of faith was mostly overshadowed by my father's dogmatic approach to religion and poor teachings through the church.

There were, however, some personally memorable spiritual events that took place in my youth which caused both fear and freedom. I had a fear of sleeping alone in my room because I swore that Jesus was appearing in my bedroom, and it terrified me to the point that I would jump if someone snuck up behind me. That fear caused me to turn off the visions at a very early age. On a more positive note, I have fond memories of times during my teenage years when we attended daily morning mass before school – mostly during Advent and Lent – and I notably had happier and less dramatic days. It was the only time in my early life where I noticed the power and freedom of morning devotion through active prayer or by reciting the Rosary. Even though I felt the power of this morning devotion during Lent and Advent, I didn't make it a practice at other times of the year. In fact, I was not comfortable talking to my parents about these experiences for fear of condemnation and so it was never talked about and I just followed what my parents did. We just went along with our 'normal' family lives.

I attended Catholic school through 8th grade, was 'schooled' in the Roman Catholic faith but left without the understanding of the fundamental spiritual truths. In fact, the only test I have ever cheated on was religion because the teachings made no sense to me. They were teaching just the stories, and the mystical truths behind the text was never explained or discussed which led me to leave the church in my 20s.

Fast forward to my 40s, when I attended a series of personal development seminars and was hooked. For the first time in my life, after being disconnected from life by consuming Prozac for 20 years, I could freely express myself and release tons of needless baggage. The first two classes made me feel empowered and energised and I wanted more. The next class of the series was occurring two days later and I was pumped and ready to go! I arrived at the class fully engaged in every lesson and then, out of the blue, on the second to the last day, I ended up in the ER after experiencing a panic attack. It was just too much on my system and I imploded. It didn't stop me, however, from attending the last session of this seminar which was given by our main speaker – a Roman Catholic priest, Father Joe Carroll. I thought, *really?* What could he possibly have to offer? To my astonishment, he commanded that stage and for the next hour completely transformed my perception about faith! His words and life experiences were so awe inspiring that it caused me to look up to the sky and call out, 'God, I don't understand you. Help me to understand.' That was the inspiration I needed to get my life back on the path.

It was 2007 and I was working as a colon hydrotherapist; running my own healing centre out of Pacifica, California, called Inner Awakening Healing Center. Within two weeks of the last seminar, my current spiritual teacher, Margaret Mary Flynn, walked through that door as a client. Little did I know that she would change my life forever. She was my gift from God.

We hit it off instantly. Margaret was honest and open, talking to me during the whole session about her life, the spiritual path, being raised in a Roman Catholic family and her mission to uncover spiritual truths. Margaret is a walking encyclopaedia of Theosophy. To this day, I don't know how one person can hold so much information in her head. Her story completely resonated within me, and my unconscious was instantly awakened. By the end of the session, I was asking her more questions and explaining my own anxiety and panic. I was hoping she could help me. Under normal circumstances, I was completely unprofessional, but Margaret knew without hesitation why she was directed to my office. In the most loving way, she handed me four Protection Decrees (Tube of Light, Beloved Mighty I Am Presence, Holy Christ Self and I Am Presence) and told me to recite and visualise them every day for thirty days. She assured me that I would no longer experience panic or anxiety. I did those mantras religiously because, remember, I was raised as a creature of Catholic habit and reciting prayers was easy. To this day, I have not had any more panic or anxiety attacks. I was free and wanted more.

Margaret is a teacher of Theosophy but was not

actively holding classes at that time. I asked her if she would start teaching again. She thought about it and shortly thereafter began teaching classes and weekly World Service in 2007 out of my office. It is now fifteen years later, and we are still going strong, reciting World Service every Wednesday. Triangles was added to our work in 2015 when Margaret took a class with Lucis Trust. Twelves was added in 2021 when Margaret discovered Steven Chernikeeff's book online, *Esoteric Apprentice*. From a humble group of five people in 2007, we have grown to twenty-four participants mostly this past year which can be attributed to active recruitment of Margaret's past students and new students with the determination to participate in Twelves. Twice a month on Full Moon and New Moon we now have one dedicated Burning Ground Twelves Zoom Group that is going strong. You can see Margaret's teachings and link to our World Service on her blog 'VioletFireCircle'.

* * *

FOR THOSE WITH a mystic or esoteric disposition, a Christian traditional upbringing will likely not only prove unsatisfactory. Dissatisfaction with teachings and a search for depth or fresh meaning often propel seekers to leave their faith for pastures new. Sometimes, and as others have already depicted, profound mystical experiences are the trigger opening up a lifelong journey of seeking and becoming, culminating in acts of service. And sometimes, the turning point comes through a dream.

KTMW (NORWAY)

. . .

IF I WERE to tell you everything that brought me to Bailey's teachings, I would have to write a book. There were a lot of happenings and synchronicities that led me to this path. I was brought up in an atheist family that before I was born had lived a life inside Jehovah's Witnesses. My grandparents were born into this belief system and my mother, being the single child of her parents, rebelled against this lifestyle, and finally they listened to her and got out of it. This caused a lot of trauma in the family. Turning your back to this means that you really start from scratch. No friends, no education (you are not supposed to get a higher education), and you have no extended family as they don't know you anymore. You are not supposed to own your house, just rent. All of this happened when my mother was twelve years old and when she was only eighteen, she got pregnant with me.

I came into this world with my hips out of place and I had to spend a lot of time in the hospital that first year. From very early on, as early as I can remember, I had an inner longing for God, something deeper and something more meaningful. I called myself a Christian and I talked my parents into baptising me when I was six years old. I was stubborn and I had some fights with my family about God that I remember very well. But nothing or nobody could really convince me that God was dead, had left humanity or was non-existent. I had a space in my home where I prayed to God, I was a member of the church choir and I had a lot of mystical experiences from an early age. When I was fourteen I studied the Bible on my own, and a crisis came when I started to read the chapter of Job. How was this possible? As I understood that the God I had an inner connection with was *not* the same as in this chapter, I didn't know what to believe anymore.

For a long time, almost a year, I had the same dream over and over again. Not every night but the same dream came randomly until I was around sixteen years old. The dream had a very special sound ambience. Later on in my life I have had similar dreams; they are quiet, but at the same time they have this special sound frequency, like a long OM, or maybe it is the bell that some talk about in Twelves? But I know when I have these dreams, that they vibrate on another level than normal dreams, and that I need to listen and be attentive.

The dream I had recurring in my youth was an octagon room with dark curtains. In the middle of the room was a crown and a sceptre. In the dream the curtains started moving due to a wind that was blowing, and I was standing in the middle of the room, rehearsing to levitate these objects with my mind.

At that point in in my life I was a very angry teenager. I was angry at my family for not believing in anything. My parents were divorced and my mother got together with a very abusive man. I was generally angry at the world. I could get so angry that I completely lost my memory about what I had said and done. So, inspired by these dreams, in combination with my intentions of becoming a better person, I started searching for answers and tools to improve myself and discovered Tarot. This led me to start training my intuition every day in the forest, to strengthen my intuition and senses to be a better Tarot reader. I studied different techniques to be more in tune with my breath, meditation, to calm down my anger and work to find a higher purpose. Many years went by where I got into paganism and shamanism. I spent a year in Denmark learning healing techniques. I understood early that I had to find my group of brothers and sisters, my coven, tribe or my soul family. But I was still on my own. I attended different meetings in different groups, and the closest I got to meeting my soul family was in a group that met regularly in the woods to take LSD and magic mushrooms. We managed to get a real connection where we had the same visions as a group. I got the same visions every time at one point. A sort of cyclic clockwork with different colours and symbols (later I came to know it was the zodiac wheel with the symbol of the rays and the planetary archetypes).

When I got pregnant with my first child at the age of twenty-two, I wanted to access another level of meaning in my life, so I searched for a serious spiritual education and found The School of Hercules. A four-year-long study of Astrology with the main focus on Esoteric Astrology. Finally, I was home. This was my language. This was what I had been searching for all my life.

It didn't take long before I had another strong dream that led me to become a student of the Arcane School. I don't have words or ways to express the gratitude I have for that training. There was so much happening inside me, so many big choices combined with my astrology studies that I just knew that I had arrived where I belonged. I was in an abusive relationship at that time, and I think my inner work in the Arcane School gave me the strength to get out of that situation and to become a single mum of two. I just knew that I was taken care of and I still feel that in the Arcane School.

I love that we can meet in Triangles without the interference of persona. That we are working as souls and that we are connected but don't know anything about each other. I also believe that it is easier this way because so many esoteric groups have been destroyed because of personalities. I have other group connections to Pythagoreans, Rosicrucians, Druids, and Pagans. I love to study everything of importance, but the path D.K gave us is the path I live and breathe in everything I do.

I have done a lot of work and I founded an Esoteric Astrology school myself. I run an esoteric centre where we have different concerts, meditations, workshops, treatments and lectures.

My whole life is about these teachings. Everything I do is about this, and being a mother for my children.

Last year I experienced in a new hardship in life. I didn't feel the inspiration as before. I felt tired and stuck, and that work, even if I loved it with all my soul, was too demanding and I was tired.

Then I received *Alice A. Bailey: Life and Legacy* by Isobel Blackthorn in the mail.

I took the teachings from the Arcane School very seriously: this is not the study of persona, but the soul. So, I never bothered reading about the lives of my inspirations, because I didn't want to mix the teachings with their personal lives. But I am so happy I did read this book. It brought me back to life again and inspiration came flowing. If Alice Bailey was a single mum and got out of an abusive relationship and still found the time to do so much service work, I could too. I must.

That first night a new dream came and it was about a vibrating star. I woke up and contacted Steven to be a part of Twelves. I knew about the group a little from before and had just attended a star meeting via Zoom. But after reading the Alice Bailey biography – the last chapter of the biography is devoted to Twelves – a link or a creative flame came back to me. So it was this book that planted that seed in me.

* * *

MANY FIND Twelves via a search for a fresh direction, the spiritual path opening up for some through an engagement with alternative spiritualities associated with the New Age movement. It would be unusual if the mother of the New Age movement, as Alice Bailey is regarded in scholarly circles, had not somehow resulted in some if not many participants walking this pathway.

CC AND JR (England)

WE STARTED on the path towards the Twelves about 2007 when we were busy at work – we are both arts-based with design degrees and we run a small café/sandwich bar in Leicester City – and CC became ill with pleurisy followed by shingles, her finger, then shingles again which left her with an immune system which could not cope with even the smallest virus or infection, or even a wasp sting! She felt devastated, down, lost physically and mentally and browbeaten and during this time we were struggling, trying to keep our 'Mom & Pop' shop going. All this happened within the space of a few months.

Doctors did what they could but CC felt an emptiness and started to look around for something, not knowing what it was she needed to fill the 'dark night of her soul' (as she says). We both looked for options and directions, CC because she felt a longing and a chasm to fill and me because I wanted to help CC out of the dark and into the light, in all senses physically, mentally and spiritually.

One weekend we visited a gathering at a Spiritual Church which I had spotted a sign for, not knowing what to expect when we arrived. It was a mixed bag of people exhibiting and talking, Spiritual Healers, Fortune Tellers, Psychic Mediums, etc. Amongst the tables was one stall selling crystals. We were drawn to the beauty and symmetry of the stones and talked to the stall-holder about what they were used for. She explained that each one of the stones or crystals had a specific purpose when used for healing. I noticed a pamphlet on the stall advertising a night-class for meditation and crystals. In fact, it was the stall-holder's night-class, which she had been running for several years. Seeing how CC's eyes had lit up, I encouraged her, and we signed up for the next term's course. We were introduced to crystal healing, pendulums and meditation, only guided meditations but a good start to encourage mental visualisations. Up to this point I had just been cruising along helping CC and hoping that this would fill the emptiness she felt. However, upon my first meditation I felt my brow chakra open and thought to myself 'this is for me'.

Luckily CC did feel better; if not wholly cured, she knew she was moving in the right direction. When the course finished, we both felt bereft, we needed to continue our growth and knowledge and were hungry to find a new path on our spiritual journey. We searched for other outlets and knowledge. I spoke to Yoga people and realised that it was a meditation for the body not the mind, and CC spotted a stall on Leicester Market selling crystals and talismans and the like. She bought some stones and spoke to the stall-holder about our predicament. The stall-holder suggested a place in Northamptonshire which had an excellent reputation with Crystal Healing: The Rose School. We visited on an open day and, liking what we saw we enrolled for the foundation course. We loved it and soaked everything up like sponges, joining in every class we possibly could.

We were introduced to full moon meditations, and although we didn't really know what they were about they became the next step on our development in mental visualisations and focused intention. We worked our way through a series of levels, spread over several years, and as we developed, we were introduced to Esoteric Healing, a higher dimensional form of healing where few if any supporting tools were used, perhaps a large crystal in the

room to set a note of energy. At this point we were introduced to the Blue Books, DK, and Alice Bailey. We applied
to join the Arcane School and were admitted as students.

CC suggested that if we could heal with our minds
someone in the same room as us, could we heal someone
not in the same room? We did some experimenting as an
independent group to the school and had a lot of success
and positive feedback. During a full moon meditation both
CC and I were impressed to create a group to do a Distant
Healing every week. We started almost immediately with
a small group of healers (fellow students) who from their
homes just before eight o'clock on a Sunday evening
would look at a list of people's names who had requested
healing, mentally connect with each other and on the
stroke of eight would start to run through a simple meditation sending healing to the soul of each person, not individually but as a group, inviting their souls to flood them
with healing light. We asked people who wanted healing
to put their names on a Facebook page and within a few
weeks we were healing thirty or forty people each Sunday
evening. Within a few months that had grown to
hundreds.

It was at this point that the Rose School thought that it
would be better to bring the distant healing under the
school umbrella rather than leaving it in our independent
hands. We felt disappointed and reluctantly decided to say
our goodbyes, feeling we had done our job and established
a solid Distant Healing system and hoping that it wouldn't
crash and burn without us. Our fears were unfounded as
the Distant Healing group is still running to this day.

However, we found ourselves in the same situation as
previously; we were bereft, and we still needed to
continue our growth and knowledge to were still hungry
to progress along the path of our spiritual journey. CC was
contacted by two Americans who were promoting the

work of DK and Alice Bailey and posting a page a day of each Blue book on Facebook pages. They said they were impressed by CC's Mandala of the day posts, which CC had been posting for several years. CC agreed to post the first of many books over the years.

We progressed with the Arcane School teachings, learning and developing, and encouraged to have a focused learning approach, to be in control of the mental, physical and emotional elements of the self, focusing upon the positive energies and to participate within life as an observer with an understanding, loving heart and a will to good. The learning and meditations continued, working with several secretaries over the years, continuing New Moon meditations and attending and even giving a talk to the annual Conference which we attended each year. We attended many meetings at the local Theosophical Society and talks from like-minded people but overall felt it was a little too biased towards the personality rather than the soul.

Then Life kicked back at us; in one year CC lost her brother and shortly after I lost my mum. CC's mum, Barbara, had shared a flat with CC's brother, and the flat was in a dreadful state and needed sorting out, and CC's Mum needed daily care, both mentally and physically. As we were the only family capable of doing this it fell to us to, and this was going to be a morning, noon and night commitment.

We struggled to try and fit everything in and work, getting up at four fifteen each morning to be ready to serve breakfasts at six, and then working through the day. CC would squeeze in visits to Barbara throughout the day as I delivered outside catering or visited wholesalers, until four o'clock each day when the café closed and we could both pay our attention to Barbara. We became exhausted, and after three years of trying, CC said she couldn't keep up with the Arcane School work and stopped corresponding with the school. I tried to continue, but without the support of CC, I too stopped corresponding.

However, we did not lose our enthusiasm for the teachings. We still attended the annual conference when possible, or attended online. We still did Full Moon meditations, CC continued to post the blue books on Facebook, but I took a more practical approach trying to work out and participate within life as an observer with an understanding, loving heart and a will to good in the real world (Arcane School teachings). Time passed and years flew bye in which we were seemingly spending most of our time attending to work, Barbara or a domestic crisis. But we did manage to have a long weekend away in 2011 and we managed to squeeze a proper fortnight in 2015, but it was shoulders to the wheel otherwise.

Finally, after a series of serious illnesses and hospital visits, it was decided to move Barbara to a care home as she had reached a stage where we couldn't provide the full-time care that she needed. We still saw her almost every day but we suddenly had extra time, although we also had a lot of catching up to do domestically, not being wealthy. JR would carry out any works needed in the house and the garden, and this had been on a fire-fighting basis and a lot of catching up needed to be done.

CC had always continued to search the world wide web and keep tabs on other esoteric groups around the world, reading and analysing their intentions and message to the world, and it was at this period in 2018 that CC happened upon the story of Twelves on the Blavatsky Bailey and Roerich Facebook page, and Steven said he had written a book about his experiences. I bought her a copy as part of her Christmas present. It was suggested on the site that Steven should attempt to start the Twelves again and CC said yes to joining even before she had read the book. Meanwhile I was happy to be a bystander deep in the practical world swamped with DIY to catch up on.

In December/January of 2019/2020 we managed to get a holiday abroad and CC suggested I read Steven's account of Twelves, and having finished reading my other books I agreed. (Obviously CC had this scheme planned otherwise why had she brought a book she'd already read). I immediately recognised the intentions of the group and the methods being utilised and agreed to become a working member of the Twelves. And so the Twelves work began.

* * *

OFTEN, the spiritual journey is one of following one direction when another opens up, then another, until you settle in, perhaps feeling you may have arrived at your destination. It's the nature of seeking, especially in contemporary society where so many paths are open to all. Many arrive in Twelves with some familiarity with Alice Bailey and the teachings. With others, it's the reverse. They find Twelves and then start to engage with the DK material.

LM (Canada)

SINCE A YOUNG AGE, I have always been attracted to the esoteric, metaphysical and spiritual world, maybe since I was twelve years old. I read books about metaphysics, but I didn't practice anything until I did a course in the Silva method, which was what started me on the meditation practice when I was about twenty-one. I didn't experience anything spectacular but I did notice that I could retain information better than before, I had better rapport with friends, classmates and teachers, and I guess in a way, I got what I wanted quite often. This practice has been part of my life, on and off since then, but I didn't make much out of it.

In 2015, I learned about Reiki, and I was fascinated by it. I studied it and practiced for my own benefit. This changed my spiritual views and started a more constant practice of meditation. It wasn't until 2018 that I met someone who introduced me to the Triangles meditation. My very first Triangle was with her and another lady, with whom I still connect daily. After a couple years of constant meditation, she invited me to the Twelves group. It was at this time when I really dived into learning more about Lucis Trust, Alice Bailey, and Twelves practice, and although I'm not a big scholar on the concepts, I enjoy the practice. I enjoy the coming together of a group of people from all over the world, from different walks of life, to heal humanity at an energetic level. How beautiful is that?

* * *

THERE ARE those who have gravitated to Twelves via an Eastern tradition. Theosophy, with its blending of Western esoteric ideas with those from the East, appeals to the esoterically minded raised in the Hindu faith. And again, out of the roots of tradition, due to an apparent chance meeting or encounter of some kind, an inner door opens and the young person becomes a seeker, and the world of esoteric meaning grows into a lived reality.

KO (INDIA)

. . .

MY PARENTS GUIDED me to yoga and meditation since childhood. Mine is an orthodox south Indian brahmin family. I am a banker by profession. At the age of twenty-four, I was introduced to a great personality, Dr M Sriramakrishna Msc Phd, whom we call Master RK. He is my mentor, guide, guru, and guided me to read spiritual books. He has included me in his mission to spread Gayatri Mantra and Gayatri Yagnam in South India. We disseminate the importance of gayatri mantra and gayatri yagnam to create a thought revolution as a solution to all types of pollutions including thought pollution. During our activities he also introduced us to the literature of Theosophy, Agni Yoga and Master DK (Alice A Bailey). We found in our research many similarities between Ancient Vedic Wisdom and this literature. Learning and Research is going on and on. The twenty-four books of DK are a guide/workbook to understand the mechanism of Cosmos in general and our Solar system in particular in a detailed way.

In 2011 I joined the Facebook group HPB & Theosophy, which had only 1500 members at the time, and started posting all important books of Blavatsky, Bailey & Roerich. Now the group consists of 8900 members. Many joined the group and accepted me as a friend and helped me to learn a lot on the Westerner's approach towards spirituality and group work.

On invitation I joined Twelves.

* * *

THE FOLLOWING contribution captures the breadth of the search for meaning and helps to put Twelves in the broader context of those spiritually minded people working hard in preparation for the World Teacher.

• • •

RB (SPAIN)

AS A TEENAGER (I am now fifty-eight) I had spontaneous Out-Of-Body experiences. This changed my life. I began a path of spiritual and existential search. One day, looking for information about these experiences in a bookstore, I saw a book on the floor that had fallen off the shelf. It was a book on Theosophy and I felt compelled to buy it. This is where my journey began. I have explored many of the world's spiritual traditions including Tibetan and Japanese Buddhism, ecumenical Christianity, Sufism, Hinduism, and Advaita. I came across the teachings of Master DK when I was living in France in 2006. I had heard of him but never read him. Until one day, in a bookstore I saw his *Esoteric Healing* in French at a very cheap price. I bought it and reading it made a great impact on me.

Today I belong to the World Teacher Trust (a foundation with roots in India, which works for the World Teacher), to Twelves and to other groups who also prepare the coming of the World Master as well as those seeking to build an Antahkarana [or inner spiritual bridge] with Shamballa.

I feel that we are living in complex times and we have to do our part to make the externalisation of the Hierarchy possible. Steven is a great motivating force. I found Steven on Facebook and his BBR group opened the doors for me to learn about the work of Twelves in its first phase and I felt that I should participate in the second phase, starting in January 2019.

* * *

THE FOLLOWING account demonstrates the seriousness and at times the almost all-consuming nature of esoteric knowledge and practice, especially for those who make this form of spirituality their work as practitioners. Sometimes, the esoteric is an 'other life' lived quietly away from the day-to-day, and at other times, it takes centre stage.

ML (Scotland)

I HAVE READ ESOTERIC /occult books since before the internet, including the Bailey material, and was brought up with Spiritualism through my mother. Not long after she passed, I got very interested in Zen Buddhism and practised with a group where I live and at monasteries and retreat places on the west coast of Scotland. I tried doing vipassana mantra etc but preferred, and still do, serene reflection meditation over a long time. Earlier to that and alongside, I have taken the B.O.T.A postal course which was founded by Paul Foster Case through the Master R as he relates in his writings. Also, Colour and Sound Meditation alongside a lot of Mental Gymnastics with Gematria Yoga of the West. So, some synthesising of both East and West as of the Trans Himalayan school. Which brought me to the Theosophical Society in my seeking which I joined 2011 in Dundee. I used to enjoy attending their meetings every two weeks on a Friday evening, until recently that is. These days they are all on view through the wonders of Zoom and YouTube.

In one of my searcher days through the now bewildering display of Occult and Esoteric literature I chanced to see the slim volume of *Esoteric Apprentice* and, having already read and pondered quite a few volumes of the blue books, I was intrigued to discover someone who had an inner contact. From there I joined the Facebook group. Although I am sceptical about such electronic platforms and their agendas, I was willing to give it a try. And knowing that Energy allows Thought to move, it would be another vehicle to express aspiration that I have and find others have within the group too. Which even from afar have formed an impression.

I would also like to add that personally I have always aspired to be part of a Group, Esoterically Speaking, rather than being alone. The connection is everything although there is a long way to go with that.

* * *

THE FOLLOWING contribution depicts an interesting route to the Bailey teachings and Twelves via her prized student psychiatrist Roberto Assagioli, founder of psychosynthesis, and demonstrates the breadth of meditation experience many in Twelves have.

LF (FLORENCE, Italy)

I HAVE BEEN on the spiritual path for about thirty years. Everything started after my father 's death, when I began to ask myself many questions about life and death. In that period, I decided to attend a yoga course and a friend of mine suggested I to go the Psychosynthesis centre in Florence, Italy, and I went there. My curiosity was captured by some courses of inner growth and my personal work began. At the Institute of Psychosynthesis I was approached by a psychotherapist and theosophist who invited me to enter her meditation group. I did not know anything in this field and at the beginning I did not accept the invitation. After many attempts by her, I got convinced and joined her group. She introduced me to the theosophical teachings and studies and taught me how to lead meditation groups. My passion for Psychosynthesis and Theosophy grew immediately and I followed this psychotherapist for many years. I started with psychosynthetic meditation and then with a creative one. In addition, I followed many Masters from different traditions. Meanwhile, I have become specialised in leading creative and angelic meditation, and in the last year, I got the opportunity to attend the school for instructors of Biodynamics Mindfulness meditation. I joined Reiki training, Master Choa Kok Sui Prana Healing training, Cabala studies, Biomechanics and biodynamics cranio-sacral school and Aura-Soma training. I am also specialised in the Angelic and Archangelic field, creating 'Angel Breath' Academy.

The Master D.K. inspires my interior work and my studies, and then my work with other people. I saw the Twelves group on Facebook 'by chance', and I felt attracted.

* * *

THE JOURNEY to Twelves has to start somewhere. For some, it's a dream or a vision, an awakening to the path, for others it's a chance encounter or a recommendation that opens the door and the process begins. From the practice of yoga, through pranic healing, it's a simple step to an awareness of the spiritual hierarchy.

JGGA (GHANA, Africa)

MY ESOTERIC BACKGROUND started with Kundalini yoga. I was then introduced to the existence and work Masters through Church Universal and Triumphant. Which led me to become a pranic healer and Arhatic yogi, working with West African Pranic Healing for a while. And I got to know more about the Masters through their courses and recommended books from Lucis Trust, Theosophy and other wonderful works on the subject. I am currently part of MindScan TM as a Meditation Mentor and Esoteric healer with the help and blessings of the Divine Truth and Our Beloved Ascended Masters.

I jumped at the opportunity when I was invited by a member of Twelves named JGG. I never miss any opportunity to be of greater service to creation, and it's a pleasure and privilege a constant channel of light. Our planet needs more light.

* * *

OUT OF THE emerging similarities among these contributions is a blending of esoteric and mystical pathways, and a transitioning through a range of traditions. The following contribution depicts a journey from Rosicrucianism, into and through various versions of Theosophy and beyond – including some less than satisfactory experiences – towards a growing appreciation of authenticity and the work of the masters of the wisdom. Yet again, Twelves represents a culmination of a decades long journey, providing an opportunity to be of service in a group that embraces without question or prejudice the diversity of backgrounds as portrayed here, a group that places a high value and strong emphasis on respecting and protecting members.

EB (France)

. . .

To INTRODUCE myself in a few words, I am female, retired for six years now, and a fervent reader of everything related to the human from a spiritual, esoteric, mystical and astrological point of view, and this has been so since I was thirty-three years old. Over time and until now (2022), my passion for knowledge and wisdom has never ceased.

From the point of view of dates: I was a member of the Rosicrucian Fraternity A.M.O.R.C. without interruption for twenty-four years, that is to say until the completion of the lessons. It was the richest period. I learned service, perseverance, self-transcendence, fraternity, and purity of intention. And I had a double-bottom vision experience. One day, I was accompanied on a walk through town. After giving alms to a beggar who looked like a young student, I saw his eyes, and was moved and it was soon after that the vision experience happened. I saw the trees in transparency in their molecules, their atoms, the road was composed of stars that were constantly moving. There was a transparency in what I saw. It only lasted about an hour. Another time, I saw white powder was coming out of my navel.

I had my first meditations with the Rosicrucian Fraternity and I persevered, followed all the monographs, even appreciating the obstacles. Brotherhood, like everywhere else, is made up of ups and downs but beyond that, we were brothers and sisters and the Masters were in my heart.

Then, following a move to another region without a Lodge, Pronaos or Chapter, I lost all contact, my studies being completed. I missed the group, so I contacted the manager of the 'Share International' group who lived sixteen kilometres from my home. Meditations were held once a week in the evening at his home. In this small group, we had the same vision of the world and formed a solid and beautiful friendship. We shared our research, our

directions, our present, and together we were keen to practise the meditations that served to transmit the high vibrations of the Masters of Wisdom for humanity. Emptying
our thoughts was the only requirement from the Master of
Benjamin Creme.

Maitreya and the Masters of Wisdom have the heavy
task of rescuing humanity, avoiding the disasters created
by its irresponsibility. To help in this, letting the energies
pass through the chakras with a mind free of all thoughts
and an impersonal attitude is enough. This meditation
brings me closer to Maitreya and I continue to do it with
my husband and sometimes a lady joins us.

Common to many of us was our intense interest in
Hinduism. With four friends we went together to Italy to
see Swami Roberto in Turin. Some subsequently followed
him, others did not, I did not. I keep the memory, however,
of marvellous Italian sacred chants, of common thoughts
of love and of the scent of roses as he passed. Many readings by Indian Masters fuelled my desire to meet one
physically and I fell in love with the Cosmic Master Sri
Sathya Sai Baba, whose video I treasured. I shed tears of
love, as I had and still have many books relating the lived
experiences of his followers. I was dying to see him in the
flesh, at his home in Prasanthi Nilayam. It was in April
2011 but I lost this possibility when he died.

A friend then told me about another Master who
taught Hinduism and who offered trips related to training,
and also one-month programs to follow each year and I
could go to His Ashram. I do not wish to mention His
name because I ceased all contact with him after seven
years of intense living. I left because I needed something
else; the lack of love and the absence of any progress both
in me and around me (it seemed) meant this Master could
not satisfy me. Some members have had very bad experiences; I haven't had any personally but my heart was

gone. I learned a lot about Hinduism that fascinated me and still fascinates me and this Master in question was an excellent speaker, extremely cultured and intelligent, of obvious strength and charisma. The kundalini shook many bodies in the assembly (including me!) and many experienced his powers. He was clairvoyant, taught the powers of the human being, made the milk flow from statuettes at home and at a distance with some of his followers, by videoconference. Well, indeed, it is extraordinary but not my goal in life, because I believe in reincarnation and in the existence of the Hierarchy, and pure and full of love for humanity. What use would 'powers' be to me (Akashic readings, remote viewing, gifts of healing and body scanning) if I did not become at least pure in body, spirit and mind and filled with a spirit of mind and filled with love? I wish for the improvement of my Being, the awakening of my Soul and joining the Awakening through the grace of the Most High, not by powers.

I suffered from this separation but legitimately, I could no longer stay. For this Master, it was about making money, and to emulate as an extension. Relationships between people had become dominant-dominated. So distraught, a long period of loneliness followed. I did not look back, trying rather hard to recover from my disappointments.

My memories brought me back to old readings which for me were pillars of wisdom. I absorbed with delight the whole series of Agni Yoga, read them and reread them, took them with me as one takes a friend, finding them consoling and inspiring. I then picked up the books of Alice Bailey, read on the internet the numerous extracts, the PDFs, the blogs concerning Master DK. Books have been very important in my spiritual progress, and the Internet now provides us with the desired information.

Deep down inside, I continued to love the transmission

meditations that brought me back to Maitreya, whose coming I never stop wishing for and in whom I firmly believe. At the same time, I am a sympathiser of a spiritual group at the head of which is a simple man who does not claim to be a Master but who is indeed one! Discreet, erudite, who offers prayers (Gayatri, songs for Maitreya, conferences) and who is based in the New Group of World Servers, whose references are linked both to Hinduism and to Héléna Blavatsky, and the violet flame. Oh, I still have so much to learn, especially to forget my disappointments and stay strong in this experience of Twelves.

I wanted to join the group created by Steven because I totally adhere to the strength of a group, and he has reliable sources of references to Master DK. He is an undeniable force of the will and the number twelve, to which I want to join. Maitreya and the Hierarchy are my path, my goal, my dearest hope for a better future for our earth and for our decaying humanity. It is said that it is by man with his feet and his hands that the future must be built, so here is my support as it is.

Often in the past I thought about starting, or finding a Triangle meditation group. There were brochures that were sent at our request, there was so much to read! The time had not yet come for me. I found the change too literary; I yearned more for a group. My previous Master gave His teachings until late at night, I was hooked on his resourceful words on the Bhagavad Gita, his own life, a really good orator watered at the source of Vedantic texts. The vibrations weren't the same. I did not continue.

Now, thanks to Facebook, I have found traces of the Triangle meditations and even better, discovered the group of Twelve.

* * *

THE FOLLOWING and penultimate contribution is unique and demonstrates the power of the internet in helping seekers find meaningful forms of esoteric service.

LFT (Mexico)

THE FIRST BREAKING point was the experience of seeing the repeated number sequences, mainly 11:11, constantly, which led me to the work of *George Barnard* and his *11:11 Progress group* and his meditation technique 'The Akashic Construct', and then also the texts from *The Urantia Book*. After that, I dedicated myself to the regular practice of meditation, and formed part of the group '*the Esenios*' in Mexico, a group dedicated to a psycho-cybernetic healing technique, formed by *Sergio González de la Garza* based on the channelled messages of his spiritual guides.

As a guide of a *Sisterhood of the Rose* group, I follow C****'s publications in his 'Portal 2012' blog, and on one occasion, a little information was shared with us about the *Brotherhood of the Star* and the *Order of the Star*, and the importance of their role in the process of planetary liberation. It was suggested we participate in the meditations of Twelves if we felt guided. This information came to me at a point in my life where I had full commitment to the energetic work; I already had a group of people dedicated to service and felt the inspiration from within to cooperate, as all seemed to connect the dots into a bigger and more organised picture.

In my personal situation, I haven't had any previous approach to the teachings of DK. However, I have gone through many key points within the spiritual knowledge that have led me to be part of this group here and now.

* * *

THOSE DRAWN to Twelves come from diverse backgrounds, but the one thing we all agree on is Steven Chernikeeff is a magnet. Through his writing, and his interactions on Facebook, he maintains a high profile. Some join Twelves, try it out and then leave. Others come and stay. They stay because they resonate with the teachings and the practice. They decide that Twelves is an authentic expression fulfilling a need and the source is pure.

PW (USA)

The Twelves activities are grounded upon the Ageless Wisdom

AS A STUDENT of the Ageless Wisdom, I was drawn to the Twelves meditation through Steven Chernikeeff's connection to the work of the Master Djwhal Khul. After reading the *Esoteric Apprentice* and 'The Temple of Light' I perceived the occult work described therein as an active service activity that was fully in accord with the Divine Plan of our Spiritual Hierarchy and, as such, it had the potential to be extremely useful.

---

1. A mist or fog, caused by emotional responses and reactions, that distorts perception of reality.

RETURNING TO TWELVES

*A*s many individuals were finding their way into Twelves, Steven and I continued our friendship while I remained separated from the group. We collaborated on the production of *Spiritual Leadership*, two booklets composed by Alice Bailey in the early 1920s. It was in the weeks following the publication of *Spiritual Leadership* that I re-joined Twelves after Steven approached me, as he had done many times before, mentioning Twelves, and telling me how much the group had grown and changed, and inviting me back. This time, sensing I had a role to play even though I had no idea what it might be, I agreed.

In my absence, Twelves had undergone something of a revolution. When I rejoined at the end of 2021, I couldn't help but be impressed by the number of participants and their loyalty and dedication. I quickly saw that the organising group were doing a tremendous job, guiding participants, hosting events and helping the group evolve.

I soon found Twelves had hundreds of members, with many Permanent Twelves groups dotted around the world. Twelves was seeding groups in Slovenia, France, Italy, Mexico and Cuba. New groups were in formation in

India. (At the time of writing, June 2022, there are 15 groups of Twelve that amount to 180 active members.) Twelves had gained that essential momentum needed to achieve the core goal of having 144 dedicated disciples in twelve groups of twelve.

As an old member, my initial orientation period was short. I went from the general discussion group into the Distant Twelves group where members begin to work in formations of twelve for meditations. From there, thanks to a vacancy, I was catapulted into a Permanent Twelve where I suddenly found myself fully committed to all the work. I was also put back in charge of the website.

Twelves work now involved the usual daily Triangle meditation and a monthly Ashram Meditation, along with the Full Moon and New Moon meditations. The Full and New Moon meditations follow the new Twelves Protocol, a very precise and lengthy meditation given in full in the next chapter. There was another ritual called Burning Ground Twelve, which was held monthly on a voluntary basis.

I was in awe of all the dedication. Despite my aspiration to be a dedicated participant, I found the workload daunting.

I have no idea how people hold down demanding full-time jobs or deal with other life commitments and participate in weekly and even twice-weekly rituals lasting a whole hour. For me, there's a psychological spill-over into my ordinary life. The meditations exhaust me. I've come to realise that it's hard to fulfil the demands of Twelves and then return to my desk and write fiction as the two worlds occupy the same inner space, the imagination. Plus, for me, an active involvement inevitably means a major preoccupation, full immersion style. Twelves isn't just something I do, I *become* it. I'm too much of a sponge.

After months of struggle, I'm settling for a quiet corner

where I can be involved in a modest way. And the beauty of Twelves is it supports folk like me who want to be involved but temporarily or permanently find themselves unable to be right at the active centre where things are hot and bubbling.

Part of me will always be the Doubting Thomas, too, largely because I had scholarly detachment drilled into me during my PhD years. Time and again I was asked if I was an adherent of the Bailey teachings, something anathema in an academic context that requires intellectual detachment. To demonstrate that detachment, I had no choice but to be critical. I had to adopt the position of impartial observer and judge. I had to evaluate, based on various criteria, teachings that were to a large degree above and beyond scholarly evaluation.

In Twelves, as mentioned above, I temper this detachment and doubt with the logic of Pascal's Wager. I have nothing to lose and everything to gain by being in Twelves with its foundational commitment to the existence of a spiritual hierarchy.

I am also aware that, as with all esoteric teachings, there's a glamour surrounding the DK teachings, one that has the potential to seep out from every page and swamp the reader in mists of illusion and deception. The harder you study, the harder you strain to understand, the more likely you are to drown in the teachings and lose perspective. The texts are not a doctrine. They are a source of wisdom, an explanation of metaphysical reality, and a guide to spiritual practice. And despite the technical language, they are laced with esoteric veils and blinds.

An esoteric veil refers to the language used to describe the ineffable. Veiling via allusion, suggestion, hints and metaphors, stimulates the imagination and is a vital aspect of esoteric teachings. Esoteric blinds refer to the concealment of hidden and secret meanings in symbols so that the average person will think the symbols mean one thing – a surface meaning – when the symbols also mean something else, something deeper, and only the genuine seeker, adept or occult student will understand that hidden meaning.

Veils and blinds are there for a purpose, helping to stimulate learning and the development of a depth of knowledge. The same stimulating metaphors and dense symbols are used in esoteric practice.

In Twelves, when we talk of the Lord of the Flame, or the Burning Ground, or when we recite invocations filled with evocative language that points to metaphysical reality, a hierarchy of being, divinity, and spiritual power, we are conjuring a metaphysical reality and making it imaginatively real, to us, and sharpening that aspect of our consciousness. Using such symbols in invocation and ritual represents the union of the path of the mystic with the path of the esotericist. It's the culmination of esoteric practice in its purest form. The aim is to harness spiritual power in the form of light. Together, each Twelve Formation creates a funnel, allowing the light to become a vortex in a process of intensification. When we unite in formation, we have the capacity to draw down this power for the benefit of all. It isn't devotional or mystical anymore, it's a formal ritual designed to make use of the collective will of the group. Metaphors and symbols are deployed for this higher purpose, that of light and love and power.

Recognising this is what draws me to Twelves.

I hold certain things to be true. It's possible to do harm, to be cruel, selfish, hateful, bitter, resentful, manipulative, self-serving, and bad if not outright evil. It is possible to be all those things which thwart growth and seek to contract a life, a worldview, a way of being. And I believe in love, wisdom, kindness, goodwill, and growth and transformation; that we can grow and change and do better through awareness and reflection and willingness.

I believe love exists.

I believe will exists.

I believe consciousness exists.

I believe that these things are both qualities and energies.

Love expands.

Awareness expands.

I believe in the existence of collective consciousness.

Added up, this basic metaphysic is probably the shortest summary of the DK teachings there ever was.

Why did I return to Twelves? Because today, humanity faces a crisis that just grows and grows and grows. We face a cleaving, a major fork in the road right in front of us, with love and wisdom and expansion, and innovation and creation on the one hand, and selfishness and contraction and destruction if not plain evil on the other. The consequences of not acting right now in the light of love and wisdom will likely be catastrophic. We face nothing short of a global emergency of our own making. Extinction is on our doorstep.

All I have just written is fundamental to me. And I'm a hardwired esotericist. A reluctant one at that because esotericism is too often both misunderstood and abused, and attracts those who relish self-aggrandisement and power for the wrong motives; and because I see esotericism as fluid, provisional, a mirror, a riddle, a labyrinth too easily becoming a maze, but also a map, a storyteller, a tool, a guide.

I have a terrified part of myself. Not only a doubter but a naysayer. Like all mystics and esotericists, I also have an awareness beyond the ordinary and the everyday, an awareness that is intuitive and perceptive. Depending on where I position myself inside my awareness, and what I'm doing in any given moment, this other self is either ON or OFF, but even when it's OFF, it's still there in the background. This gives me a double vision, a double voice. I can project one or the other or maybe both.

I would call this beyond-the-ordinary self my best self. Others call it the higher self or soul. I'm sixty years old. What with one thing and another, I've allowed this connection with my best self to get floppy sometimes. I've been caught up in the dross – ill-health, family issues, conflicts and sagas, not to mention the pandemic. Then Twelves comes knocking and says, hey, you've got a soul too, you know (in case you've forgotten), and we need you.

Oops.

Shouldn't I have been meditating twice daily already? Aren't I in fact just the worst meditator? I'd rather knit or count beads or something. It just isn't me. Or so I think.

But then I do a meditation, especially one live and hosted on Zoom, and bang, I'm there, doing it, totally focused, attention unwavering. I'm not a fake or an imposter after all. This stuff feels real. And the naysayer goes quiet.

Then, the meditation is over and I get on with my life and I doubt again and I naysay. Many times I have worried I'll lose my ordinary life to it. How will I be creative? How will I write fiction? Won't this swallow me whole?

All my worries are founded.

How will I integrate Twelves into my life? How will it change me? I don't have the answers, but I do know that despite all my misgivings, it's great to be back. For me, Patrick Chouinard captures beautifully the joyful essence of Twelves:

 White magic is the unifying spirit and matter, and bringing the spirit down into the material

world, infusing it and transforming/transmut-
ing it. This is the work we are doing in
Twelves. This is the work of the soul – which
links Spirit with the personality (right into the
physio-etheric level) – and of the disciple. All
of us have been brought together at this time
for a reason. It's unprecedented I think for so
many disciples to be connected on the physical
plane. (And not just in the DK community.) As
the 'Rules of the Road' state: we travel not
alone. We are supported, sustained and
strengthened by our co-disciples and we have
(or can have) what DK calls 'the comradeship
of the Path'. We discover the beauty of the
group life in joyful service together.

TWELVES CORE GROUP –
ORGANIZING TWELVES

*T*aking on the website management role put me back at the centre of operations. I was added to the Core Group of organisers and quickly gained an understanding of the complexities and workload many had taken on. Membership was in the hundreds. At the time of writing, the main discussion group has well over a hundred members. Independent Twelves groups dotted around the world easily add another hundred to the group.

Twelves members were now performing daily Triangles meditations, and Full and New Moon meditations using a new Twelves protocol. Vita had helped give birth to the Burning Ground Twelves protocol and wrote the commentaries to go with it. Twelves had been using a City Invocation to help dissipate glamour in the city triangulation of New York, London and Moscow, which was included in the BGT meditations that were at that stage occurring monthly. So much activity meant a lot of organising and a lot of discussion as to how best to streamline the work.

And still, Twelves remained in flux. As Vita acknowl-

edges, the 'protocols, especially BGT, will change. Whatever work we do might be obsolete tomorrow but serves
as a needed stepping stone in our learning and practice'.

Absorbing this new and thriving Twelves reality, I
again felt like an imposter. Vita helped pour light onto my
problem. 'With regards to you being 'new and a beginner'
- that is *your* thoughts! You forget how much you have
actually taken in with your PhD and your Alice Bailey
books. That s all stored within you. Your lower mind
might not remember but it is all there and all available to
you. On that level you are a powerhouse! And it is from
this supra-conscious aspect that the work is done.'

I saw straight away that she was right; I have a habit of
underestimating myself. Maybe it dates back to an event
when I was twelve years old. I'd scored top marks for a
test and I was so overjoyed I told my friends. I thought
they would be pleased for me. Instead, their response was
a crushing, 'So, what? You're just bragging?' I was put in
my place, cut down to size, forced to negate my joy. It's the
Australian way that teaches children early on that they
must always be or pretend to be humble and major in
being 'average' and 'ordinary' and 'mundane'. Excellence
is anathema except in sport. More likely, it's a tendency I
was born with.

Vita went on, and her insight is worth quoting as it
speaks not so much of me, as of a danger with esoteric
work of this kind:

66 Furthermore, you are *ideal* for Twelves and
especially for Burning Ground Twelves. Most
people think they need to *do* something, while
the service rendered in Twelves and BGTs is to
be a channel. Through our intent and will-to-
serve, and through making ourselves avail-

able, the ashramic workers (devic etc) will use that funnel that reaches up but is anchored on the earth plane to do *their* work. We are to do....NOTHING, just hold that intent, do the task at hand and help in visualising, which then become directives for ashramic workers, their direction, THEIR task. All this being an 'expert' is pure illusion. What is needed is to hold that intention and that emptiness or neutrality without adding one's own ideas or mixing it with other rituals. The expertise in Twelves comes from much higher sources and we are all babies. So don't throw the baby out with the bathwater! In this case you are the baby! You are precious and you are needed. Each of us are needed, desperately needed.

I took heed, but being in Twelves was never going to be a straightforward path for me. The soul is subtle, the behind the scenes operative, leading the personality forward. I respond magnetically to Twelves, and yet my personality remains a confusing melting pot of thoughts, feelings, sensibilities, frailties and foibles, as well as strengths and attributes. Sometimes I think I must walk the spiritual path in spite of myself and certainly not as a result of any devotion or striving on my part. That even someone as fickle and doubtful as me remains in Twelves speaks of the group's power to attract and hold, and to its purity of motive and method.

As Patrick Chouinard notes:

Love, trust and loyalty are the foundations of a spiritual group and through our unity and shared purpose (all of which keeps us together despite differences, defects and temporary clashes) we can become a channel for love and light of uncommon magnitude. These foundations are only possible if we get to know each other a little (I have befriended my Triangle partners).

That means opening up somewhat (chiefly our hearts). That doesn't mean getting entwined in each other's personal lives and talking overmuch about our personal problems with each other (though of course we should reach out to each other when there is a real need and should help each other where we can) and especially not talking about the problems or defects of others in the group (real or imagined) unless it is for a constructive purpose. I heard a great expression: be personable with impersonality. It's about finding the right balance.

Our goal I think is to see each other as souls (focusing on the good); to believe in and encourage each other, and to demonstrate that ideal of unity (what good is our idealism if we can't actually demonstrate it in life).

Being mindful of the service we can do should help us overlook perceived or annoying defects or differences. Personality reactions (i.e., ego reactions) have to be put aside for the sake of the work and shared purpose take precedence - all the while visualising the lines of golden light connecting us (our hearts in particular).

TWELVES IS group work and groups are never easy places, especially for someone impulsive and outspoken like me. Better to be silent, keep your own counsel, the least said the better. I am noisy, messy, and barrel in wanting to fix things, make things function better. I'm a communicator, a chatterbox, verbose, longwinded, full of lengthy stories about all sorts. Concise never entered my makeup. I'm not therefore great in groups. And I'm excruciatingly aware of this. Finding myself in a group of people majoring in reserve and silence and careful communications makes it even worse for me as I feel I have to fill that silence. When Vita asked me to take over the website and I was thrust into the core of the organisation, I knew I faced a ton of lessons in that group.

After a few fraught months in which the website crashed thanks to Malware and I spent two weeks frantically rebuilding it using a different server, my involvement in the Core Group became too intense and I was nearing burnout. As soon as I saw the signs that I was getting much too frazzled, I took time out.

Sometimes, a group is better off when certain key figures put themselves on the periphery or when members withdraw for a while. An organising group of volunteers dealing with weekly events and the limitations and frustrations arising from the Facebook platform, a group that also discusses the next evolutionary steps, the next point of advancement, a group doing all of this using Messenger chat which has a habit of making communications linear, fragmented and abrupt; the Twelves Core Group deserves credit for their organising abilities alone, as all this is no small feat.

I re-entered Twelves with a host of misgivings and apprehensions thinking I really wasn't cut out for the work and I would leave, sometime soon. I was cautious and didn't want to get too involved, preferring only to participate. I thought I would play a minor role looking after the website. After the Malware saga, as I re-created the website, I began to own it, and I knew that was necessary. That someone, me, needed to manage the website as it is central to everything Twelves is doing. And as I created page after page after page, the website gave me a fuller understanding of Twelves. It was that fuller understanding that led to the creation of this book.

THE TWELVES PROTOCOL

$\mathcal{F}$ull participation in Twelves is quite a commitment. The monthly Full Moon and New Moon meditations, performed within a twelve-hour window to either side of the exact conjunction, means participants can choose a time of day that suits. These meditations are performed in groups of twelve in Twelves formation following the new protocol, which is long and there is a lot to absorb all at once.

The Disciples Invocation (detailed in the following chapter) needs memorising and at first, I found I needed a cheat sheet, both for the meditation itself and the invocation. The aim is to practise the meditation often enough that the process is second nature and moved through with ease. And moving through with ease means not only do you know what you are doing, you are able to visualise the entire process, holding the Twelve Formation steady in your imagination as you recite the invocations and meditate on a seed thought, all the while being aware that you are connecting to the ashram and enabling the harnessing and direction of spiritual energy. Sustained focus and concentration for up to an hour are required which is why advanced meditators are sought for involvement in Twelves. Knowing this, I was always going to find it hard.

Team members, including Murray and Vita, put their minds together to create a new Twelves protocol and I have included it here in full, as there is no better way to understand the process.

THE TWELVES PROTOCOL

as it appeared on the Twelves website, April 2022

There are seven steps in the process. In the past these stages were undertaken in a standing upright position, but this is not a requirement anymore. However, some workers choose to stand during the Vortex phase. The worker gets ready by meditating in a sitting position, with either legs crossed or with both feet on the ground. The process from start to finish will take about one hour.

Undertake the meditation as close as possible to the exact moment of the full or new moon or Festival times. If that is not possible then choose a time as close as possible to the exact moment within a twelve-hour window leading up to the precise time.

1. ENTERING SACRED SPACE

This requires individuals to be fully responsible and, apart from the obvious cautions about drugs, alcohol etc. being incompatible with the work, it is important for co-workers to be ready with *intent*. This means preparation of one's being at least 3 days before a Twelve and adhering to right action in one's daily meditations and invocations. A calm, focused mind is required for this work and, most important, setting aside all personal 'stuff' at the door. Be aware that the space you are entering is now a sacred space.

Assuming that the worker is now able to maintain a focus and is trained in the art of Triangles, emotionally and mentally still, has read and understood the *Esoteric Apprentice* (a requirement freely available from our website) and is clear that personal issues have to be set aside whilst undertaking this service activity, then the worker can move on to the next stage.

2. STANDING IN THE LIGHT AND THE CIRCLE OF PROTECTION

Whenever group work is undertaken under the auspices of the Ashram, protection is invoked. So, in a larger group setting such as the Twelves Work, we can be assured of protection on the group and likewise for individuals.

It is helpful to visualise the whole group present and standing in the Light, with co-workers outlined and surrounded by light, rather than as a specific person, male or female etc.

When the time has come, ideally at the synchronised time (though this is not a strict requirement, as long as within a twelve-hour window leading up to the stipulated time) visualise and connect with all Twelves members and with your Triangle co-workers, in anticipation of joining the larger group formation.

When occultly ready 'step' forward one pace to symbolise stepping into the group. When the connection between the group members feels firm, 'hear' all recite with you the **Great Invocation** followed by **three OMs** affirming that protection on all members, on the group, on the supporters and the work offered in service through the group in formation. See the circle of protective light expanding ten meters (thirty feet) or more beyond all.

3. EXECUTING THE TWELVE FORMATION

Now visualise the first 'North' Triangle members 'stepping' forward one pace and 'activating' their triangle in readiness for the work ahead. The links between triangle members are not static but are 'alive'. Now visualise the second 'South' triangle stepping into the space. Their triangle floats above the first triangle and then is lowered upon it. This process is then repeated by the third ('East)' Triangle and then the fourth ('West') Triangle thus completing the Twelve Formation.

VISUALISE your Triangle partners and all co-workers in the Twelve Formation and feel the soul light and soul love weld you into a unity. When the formation is thus executed, 'hear' all reciting together with you **The Great Invocation** followed by **three OMs**.

When advancing in this work, the worker will definitely feel the stages of connection, which can be quite dramatic, occultly speaking, when the Triangles merge and the Twelve Formation is being completed.

During this stage feel the group being energetically charged, as the anticipatory build-up of energy is reached by the group as a whole. This is the point when connection with the Ashram may be made. The anticipatory build-up of energy can be palpable and even, sometimes, seen.

This can impact your daily life. A sense of being energised, as occultly understood, may remain with you in unexpected ways and can be life changing. This has often been described as a magnet with one end representing self and the other the Ashram, once the link has been established. It 'pulls' the individual. No doubt many will have felt this in other esoteric activity, and it really intensifies with advanced group work in service to the race/the earth. Do not be alarmed! Hidden hands guide the group and its work.

4. INVOKING THE VORTEX

Now the connection is made. Visualise your Triangle partners and all co-workers in the Twelve Formation recite the **Disciple's Invocation** followed by **three OMs**. Visualise the Vortex descending into the centre of the group. At this point some may sense other beings around the Twelves. Acknowledge their presence but do not engage with them. It is their task to work with the Vortex, to provide protection and assistance.

On every single occasion when a physical Twelve Formation was undertaken a Great Deva attended at the mouth of the Vortex. If individuals sense or recognise this, they can appreciate this Presence, but they should stay focused on the work at hand, there is no need to invite it over for coffee. Please do not engage; but a silent 'thank you' is enough, as all serve in their specific roles to make this a success.

5. RADIATING OUT

Visualise as you repeat The Great Invocation, Light, Love and Power descending through the Vortex, down into the centre of the Twelve, into the NGWS, the Triangle Grid and out into the world.

While reciting **The Great Invocation** followed by **three OMs,** stay focussed on your Triangle and its seamless insertion into the Twelve Formation as it acts as a channel/funnel through which Light, Love and Power descends and radiates out into the world. Hold this for 10-15 minutes.

6. LIFTING AND DISSOLUTION

After approximately ten to fifteen minutes, visualise the Light slowly dissipating and lessening. See each Triangle now slowly and purposefully rising above the other three Triangles and dissolving beautifully, quietly and peacefully into the ether

Give thanks to the angelic, devic and ashramic workers who made this work possible and for the opportunity to serve in this way. You might want to finish with reciting an Invocation of your choice, followed by three OMs.

7. INTEGRATION

Take time to integrate this experience afterwards to allow all bodies to readjust.

LIVING THIS PROCESS

It is important to 'live' this process and keep focused on the reality of what we are all undertaking together. The keywords to integrate are:

- INTENT
- FOCUS
- DELIVER

THE YEAR 2025 beckons and all must advance group work NOW. After 2025, a new teaching will emerge as the third part of the Ancient Wisdom outlined by HPB and AAB and others. That is not the task of this group. In Twelves, disciples have come together to advance and experiment with group synthesis and group action in a specific formation – a band of brothers and sisters. The Call has gone out and disciples have responded. Are you ready for the task at hand?

* * *

IT SHOULD BE clear from this outline how formalised Twelves work is. The development of hour-long rituals out of the original Triangles meditations found in the DK teachings and founded by Alice Bailey represents a significant advancement along theosophical lines. I asked Steven Chernikeeff if he knew of any other similar work being done in the world at this time and he told me if there is, he hasn't come across it.

DISCOURSES AND THE
DISCIPLE'S INVOCATION

*W*hile Triangles work comes straight from Alice Bailey and DK, the Twelves Ashram Meditation, the Twelves Protocol and the Burning Ground Protocol have been developed following the instructions of The Initiate via Steven Chernikeeff. It wasn't until I started engaging deeply with *Discourses* that Twelves took on its real significance, and my respect for Steven grew stronger knowing how difficult it is to find yourself in telepathic rapport with or open to impression from an intermediary being, and remain humble. Steven acknowledges in *Esoteric Apprentice* that in his younger years he did succumb to the almost inevitable inflation and glamour that comes with holding such a unique position. And little wonder since Steven is, by extension, another intermediary in a great chain of being.

Discourses traces what Steven has come to know about The Initiate and details the teachings Steven has received in chronological order. Steven has identified The Initiate as being of Chinese origin in the Qing Dynasty and was a senior monk and Buddhist meditation master in the Qing Province. The Initiate lived in Qinghai near the Tibet border and was a regular visitor to Tibet. Steven believes he was attached to the Kumbum Monastery where he taught in the late 1800s and early 1900s, striving to establish esoteric principles on earth. The Initiate is an assistant to the Master Koot Hoomi and others in the Brotherhood of the Star. He has assisted in the founding of Twelves in order to help externalise the hierarchy. The Initiate came to London and met Steven and co-founder Robert and stayed in Robert's house for about an hour. When asked by Steven 'how did you find us', he told the men, 'A star in the sky guided me, and I followed it'. In the 1970s, the decade before the foundation of Twelves, Steven wrote a book of meditation seed thoughts which he later realised were a collaboration with The Initiate. The connection has grown stronger ever since.

To give a taste of The Initiate and an insight into the significance of a core invocation in Twelves work, following The Disciple's Invocation itself is an extract from *Discourses*.

The Disciples Invocation

May the Flame of the One find the Crucible of your being

May the Mighty One issue forth from on High

May Love eternal and Love inclusive rule over all

Let the Flame spin upon the Way

Let the Light stand revealed

Let the seeker become the Rose

May the tide of illusion be turned

May the Great Work be completed

May the White Ones issue Their Ultimatum

Let the Ultimatum be heard by those who have ears to hear

Let them have insight and knowledge that they may understand

Let them choose aright and with free will

And in so choosing let Peace come to Earth

* * *

May the Flame of the One find the Crucible of your Being

As WE JOURNEY through this ashramic Invocation I would ask that you use your intuitive faculties as best you may for much of what I have to say is addressed to those realms.

The first line, as is apparent, consists of a recognition that before our journey begins, we must alight the flame that is a part of the One in our innermost being, and so the invocator cries aloud that from that mountain most high a flash of light may be seen to issue out and find and inspire that part of man which we call his being or that which IS. We cry aloud that a small part of Him may be stirred in all aspirants, that it may be flamed and nurtured into the LIVING FLAME.

And so, we venture into the test of material life and so prove ourselves to become in truth Sons and Daughters of God in the crucible of our being. This line represents primordial fire, that spring from which life is created and moulded. It is a call to the innermost of each to BECOME and so begin their quest for the Grail.

There is a Law of this world cycle that the Head of the Spiritual Hierarchy of this planet, The World Teacher, must re-emerge into the world of men. This event, that He may have a tangible presence, is being worked for and towards by all Hierarchical workers. This line:

May the Mighty One Issue Forth from On High

...is the invocator's recognition of this fact and his welcoming of The World Teacher Presence into his life and his world – the world of men. As we say this

In line with intent let us picture The World Teachers Light radiating from the Mountain out into the peoples of the world. Let us not forget that we create the conditions for His return. Now we come to the line that finishes the first stanza off:

May Love Eternal and Love inclusive Rule over All

THESE WORDS EXPRESS what the coming of The World Teacher represents for humanity. His keynote is LOVE and His message INCLUSIVENESS, that inclusiveness that holds no barriers and encompasses all. This first stanza sets the tone for the Invocation, it recognises three important facts:

1. That we all have within us a part of the One which awaits the Call Home;

2. That The World Teacher shall re-emerge and shall descend from on High;

3. That Love is eternal and barrierless and that the invocator recognises that inclusiveness must rule over all for the Plan to work out.

Therefore, this first stanza is introductory and assumes

the three facts above. A point of tension should be held in between each stanza. Stanzas 1 and 3 are inward and upward, stanzas 2 and 4 are downward and outward as in the breath. The last line is bringing to conclusion the 'work' of the invocation and symbolically of the present cycle.

As we begin to explain this second stanza, we should realise that it has a reflective quality. The first stanza is a request to the Source of all Life that man may recognise and understand the three basic facts above. Now the invocator has set the tone, he has offered his request and it has gone forward with power. Now let the invocator 'bring down' and 'send forth' on a ray of light the response:

Let the Flame Spin Upon the Way

THIS REFERS to the monadic state, and although this line cannot be fully comprehended till after the third initiation, I shall try to explain in a simple manner, for I do not wish to unnecessarily complicate things. The invocation refers to the Destroyer aspect which burns away the dross of illusion and

transmutes it in its action. The Way is both symbolically the spiritual pathway and correspondingly the *way* to the head centre. This brings us automatically to the line:

Let the Light Stand Revealed

...AND OF COURSE, the Light of the Soul can only reveal itself when the dross has been *shattered* by the Flame. The invocator now commands:

Let the Seeker Become the Rose

THE ROSE IS an ancient symbol often referred to as 'The Rose upon the Cross'. The Rose is attainable through the crucifixion of matter. The Rose is symbolic of the heart centre wherein Realisation is found. The World Teacher again is found here as the symbol of the Heart.

The heart of humanity is at the moment shielded from the light by illusion. Instead of revealing The World Teachers Glory to his fellow beings, man has held in his midst but a low reflection, that of sentiment. The World Teachers Light no longer beams out into the world of men, yet it slumbers awaiting that Great Day when the veils fall. On its own level only can it now shine. However, amass your cries, let it peal forth:

May the tide of Illusion be turned

MAN MUST CONQUER his emotions and begin to emerge into the light of his Soul. By clear thinking responsible men and women may turn the tide by allowing the Soul to be the master. All may be a party to the push that is now taking place both on the inner and outer planes. The great transmutative work must proceed:

May the Great Work be Completed

MAN MUST BLEND his lower self into the higher, thus transmuting base passions into higher attributes. This is

the Great Work, the path to the thousand petalled lotus.
Man must synthesise his being, becoming a Son of God
and thus fulfilling his eventual destiny. The time has come,
friends, when the choice has to be made:

May the White Ones Issue Their Ultimatum

THE CHOICE of humanity is a response to the Hierarchical
output now taking place. This line indicates that the invocator recognises this fact and that he consciously says and
accepts that the time has come for Externalisation and the
re-emergence of The World Teachers Cosmic Principles
and he welcomes this in intoning this line with meaning
and power.

All of humanity may participate in these events. Individuals must choose between the dictates of the Soul and
the forces of materialism. We may cross the divide, or we
will have to wait for another opportunity.

Let those who constitute the ready 'hear' this Ultimatum and recognise the present opportunity:

**Let the Ultimatum be heard by those who have ears
to hear**

LET each listen for the note in his own way but, there is
only one conclusion to be reached – the moment of crisis
has emerged whereon the Hierarchy shall emerge
triumphant:

**Let them have Insight and Knowledge that they may
understand**

TO EACH, in his own way, will be given the insight and knowledge; no one (none in original) will be missed. When the Mighty One returns each shall see and hear and each shall accept or reject, this is the Law:

Let them choose Aright and with Free Will _

THE INVOCATOR INTONES this line that all may make the right inner choice, the choice of their Soul which ever strives for the light. Let the invocator solemnly speak these words in the hope that few may turn aside from the light and enter the dark pathway. Free will must and will be retained by all, none may claim other than this:

And in so Choosing Let Peace Come to Earth

LET this end line be said in a manner that resembles a *striking forth*; let it go forward into the world to work for peace. Mankind must make changes for himself, he must prepare the Way. The conditions are set, information can be circulated around the world in little or no time; an action in one country far away is common knowledge a little while later. Man has the tools to recreate his world.

The World Teacher awaits and is preparing for His re-emergence. This point shall be achieved and is being achieved right now. Even as I talk to you today, my Brothers are active.

You who will read these words are entrusted with the task of using this Invocation in conjunction with, and peripheral to, the Invocation* that you have been given some time ago.

These instructions are of a very simple nature and are designed to be of use to the general interested public. Those amongst you who are trained esotericists shall no doubt see beyond my simple words and shall find, with study, the deeper significance.

This invocation is especially potent at this time in rallying the forces of good to the aid of a struggling humanity. It is used frequently by those who constitute the Second Ray Ashram, each Ray having an Invocation which when said in a combined manner effects certain results which facilitate an easing of tension and an accentuating of spiritual values.

The invocation that is called the Great Invocation contains *tones* of combined Ray invocations and should still be the main tool and is used as such (in a different scale) by us.

The invocation that we have given to aid workers in the externalisation process is a translation only which changes on different levels, a hint is given here. Let the student keep foremost in his mind these four things:

1. The World Teacher shall Return
2. The Soul must be Master
3. Illusion must be Pierced
4. The Choice must be Made

Let none be fearful, no man good and true need fear the Ultimatum for it is a crisis of the Soul. All who are sincere, although they may not realise at this time the facts here written, shall be *saved* and borne up into the arms of the Lord. The World Teacher awaits, shall we not hasten His coming? This great event shall become actual to your everyday eyes and ears. This wonderful opportunity awaits all men. Take up then the challenge for the time is set although no man shall know the hour nor the day, His coming is certain.

* * *

IT OCCURS to me there are levels of dedication in any group. You can read The Disciple's Invocation off a script. You can rote learn the TDI and repeat it verbatim. You can study TDI and gain an understanding of the meaning of each line. You can tune into the meaning of each line as you recite. And you can tune into the meaning as you recite while also directing your attention in the manner described above. And finally, you can tune in, recite, direct your attention all at the same time as you hold in your awareness the circle of protection, your triangle, the Twelves star, the vortex of light, all of it at once. And in so doing, observe and experience the process. That's the goal, and it takes skill and lots of practise to achieve it.

THE TEMPLE OF LIGHT

$\mathcal{T}$he following extract from *Discourses* was written by The Initiate and informs the ethos of Twelves. When Vita returned to Twelves in 2020, she had in her possession a copy of this piece, which she had kept for over two decades. At the time, she thought she was the only one who had it, as Steven had managed to tuck his copy away in a folder on his laptop somewhere, and *Discourses*, which includes Temple of Light, had not been published. It was most likely Vita's prompting that caused Steven to go digging in his files.

It is clear that Vita recognised the significance of the piece in her possession, how central it was to Twelves work, and in that mysterious fashion that so often happens to people who follow the esoteric way, it was this recognition of significance that caused Vita to dedicate herself to advancing Twelves, drawing on The Temple of Light in the formation of the new Burning Ground Protocol.

Rather than directing the reader to *Discourses*, with the author's permission I am quoting the TOL passage here in its entirety as it is the single most important piece of writing informing the group, and it cannot be adequately paraphrased or summarised.

OUR CALL

The moment of capture, in My disciple's eye of that glancing light as it is in Our domain, that is the moment of awakening to Our Call. The journey from those centers of Being is long and arduous, for Us, and the earth beckons still. That light descending filters through Our centers, through the layers of being, to the centers of earth.

Hear Our Call to come to the Wheel and become part of that journey of light. Hear Our Sound so that your apparatus becomes a channel clearer still for Our vibrations. It is in this knowledge, in this understanding that is found the Pearl – search then your structures for My Presence for I stand at the Gate of the Temple of Light beckoning you further still for this light to descend. To mix and integrate Our higher vibrations with the coarser matter requires stillness and perseverance.

Tending to the bodily structures is essential in the transference of patterns of light from Our Chalice. Much work has been achieved on Our side to bring this Ray of Light into manifestation and you, in your turn, have trodden this path to become interpreters of light. From its source of solar manifestation this lighted way seeks an easy conduit, a conduit made up of discipleship matter to facilitate the flow of energy through to the last staging post. This solar connection must be understood, for it is the source of Our Life.

Harken to the Note! Dear friends in the work, you are part of that journey of light, a span of the bridge which emanates from the far reaches of our solar system within the body of a great and wondrous being, stepped down in ever coarser (if I may use such a term) limitations to reach those centers and places on earth. This line of intent, from the spark to the flame, is a living Bridge of Light whereupon our Master may cross. This absolute activity requires each of us to dedicated activity and response to the clarion call. From the crown to the root, from the solar to the earth and from the divine to the mundane flows everlasting life.

Twelves must be likened to a Temple of Light with an outer and inner court, a sanctum, and a corridor of light encircling. To enter requires dedication, bravery, and discipline for the building of light requires exact foundations if it is to be of use to Us. The transmission of lighted force through the upper triad and the sturdy disposition of the lower quaternary is essential for the manifestation of the lighted way. The disciple will be less disturbed if the inner and outer manifestation in form is attended to exactly if due preparations are made.

From Our Centre, light can then be manifested, and a conduit achieved which will allow the temple's structure to become resilient and receptive to the energies which We will send and manifest. This structure of light shall utilise each disciples' centers (according to their propensity) and in summation shall multiply the energy for connection to earth's centres. This combination of lighted way, from higher to lower, acts like a beacon on inner planes for added impulse and work. It is seen from afar and attended to by beings of light who are drawn to utilise and aid Us at this time.

This united and concerted effort then unleashes a final, from Our point of view because it descends into matter and its kingdoms, Rays of energy through a manifested group of trained disciples rather than through more diverse structures as has heretofore been the case. That work, of course, will be increased and Our work through the great centres of human endeavour; politics, medicine, sciences, psychology, the arts, charitable endeavours of various hues, religious institutions (a work of reconstruction and focus) and with all people who work with the energy of Goodwill and are responsive, if only slightly, to Our Rays but who have, definitely, a response to their souls beating and unfolding. Our work continues on all planes and with all manifestations to raise the vibrational and transmissional activity preceding the Return. The process of this group work is twelvefold in differentiation and can be likened to the seasons, each season broken down and differentiated by three phases:

THE APPROACH

Dear workers in the light the first of these is *preparation*, the essential prerequisite of our work together. Preparing the light body three months before the formation of a Twelve is essential work well done. When the soul has made its decision to work in this way, an initial stream of light connects the worker with the Ashramic hub, and information, and preparatory energy is on hand. It is possible, of course, for less time to be utilised but three things will occur: the first is the worker will be useful but less congruent, the second is the worker will have less initial Ashramic energy, and the third is the withdrawal will be more abrupt.

The second of these is *congruence*. This phase, if I may so use it, energetically entwines the Ashramic energies with the light body of the worker in such a way as to make the facilitation of energy that much easier. One month before a formation a blending will have taken place, on subtle levels, not always consciously realised, and deep movement and realignment is possible. This phase, I counsel, is the most important for the individual worker to be the most effective he can be to Us. In this time may We impart energetic information to workers which relates to

their linkage to the Ashram, this information will sometimes *surface*, if I may use this phrase, at this stage or later,
it matters not, but the information is given.

The third of these is **assimilation** into the group formation. The worker having aligned, connected, and blended
with the particular Ashramic linkage that they individually have with Us, steps forward for the work ahead. This
should be undertaken in a quiet way with focused contemplation and linkage. It is *before* this phase that We are with
you and *at* this stage that Our workers come together for
Ashramic group work.

The worker no longer is an individual working with
others but an essential component in the formation of light
that approaches Us in service. This connection is greater
than any individual sum or any individuals working in
cooperation, great though that work is to Us, but a critical
combination of energetic force which is greatly useful to
Us on a conduit of light, focused and powerful, redeeming
and loving.

THE AWAKENING

Brothers, the first of these is **connection**; both horizontal
and vertical connection of individual centers into
a *mass* center formed at the periphery of the Ashram. This
focus of energy, talismanic in effect, magnetically aligns
the Ashramic *pull* with a line of intent. The individuals'
centers have, temporarily, become a vehicle for the formation's combined focus and, more importantly, for Us to
weld the formation into a united Temple of Light. The
connection of the stream of energy creates, firstly a web of
light, secondly an encirclement of light and thirdly a
channel of light – mark these words well.

Radiating pulses are used for protective purposes by
Ashramic workers to secure the light field, this is why

such potent group work should *always* be under Ashramic guidance and sponsorship; with this group's case warranting a special focus from Us to further substantiate the group's effect on the inner planes. A great experiment in group potency arising from a long line of intent, woven with care and with cosmic timing.

The second of these is *application* of sources of energy and power to provide linkage with the three main centers; Shamballa, Hierarchy and Humanity, to be the grounding station, the last in a very long line of light promotion down a line of intent, and so the gateway opens, and the Star shines forth.

To apply esoteric principles, I talk not of books here, to daily life and to summate this in conscious awareness and application to the discipleship group task is a service to Us indeed. Application, then, of lines of power sequentially laid one to the other, brings about a force-field of upward, energetic expression leading to the third aspect.

The third of these is *response*, the disciples' invocative call is heard most high and a response is threefold; the first is in the previous phase where beings of light are sent by Us to protect and prepare both individuals and the group whole for the work of vortex. The second is of response from Ashramic workers who are trained especially for this group work and who are adept at utilising energy fields arid centers of individuals who bring with them a complexity and require trained attention by Ashramic workers who help weld them into a group dynamic.

The third is of planetary and solar response and the stepping-down process of energy transmission. This work is not of group-directed power but of committed interaction and conscious cooperation between the Brotherhood and its members on earth, keep this in mind at all times and enclose it within your hearts.

THE OUTPOURING

My Workers in the Light the first of these is *integration*; that blending with the Rays of Energy which brings about a synergistic process, a blending with Ashramic Hierarchical force which strengthens the vessel of light to receive Our septenary Rays of Downpouring and the integrative nature of the formation creates a light-swell of force which permeates the group existence and reinforces the web of light. This process enables Us to reach the earth with an intensity of love, light and power heretofore unknown. Now My workers are refined in their integrative working with the group structure and the vehicular nature of this entwining and convexing of the funnel to receive Our power. The second of these is *communion* with these lighted beings as they pour forth Their Rays into and through the structured Temple of Light. This is the next phase so oft talked about to appear at the end of this century and to go forth as a divine science of light into the next.

As understanding of interpretation hastens a lighted way shall be precipitated. Communion is a summation of the other stages and a culmination of individual, group and extra-group forces which now channel Hierarchical energy through various structures on Our side to the funnel for onward transition for divine purpose.

The third of these is *transmission* of energy, effected and directed from Our side for purposes of world change and world transfiguration. The effects of this stage shall be manifold – for the healing of nations, cities, and popula-tions, for the lighted beings to further build the bridge of light – so promised, so near; to enable and enforce the Rays here present, to align and enlighten the fields of light that entwine the world, to reach and touch soul levels of consciousness with focused intent and to enrich the outpouring of loving energy from the Ashramic Star. In this transmission are the seeds of love and light and power and can carry the particles of response to human need. This transmission phase gives The Call to many through Our apparatus, a linkage stretching from afar, may it be so.

THE WITHDRAWAL

The first of these is *maturation;* the phase whereupon the light is fixed in the disciple's heart and eye and whereupon the outpouring has completed its task, this phase has seen the power and the light unleashed and STAND. From above, so below. The forces begin to disengage from the atomic structures above, so allowing the lighted field to begin to slow its outpouring from a stream to a trickle. The Work is complete, and the maturation of the Work sees the beginning of the withdrawal phase. The lighted brothers complete their work by sounding certain notes which find a response in the Ashramic workers who attend the Twelve on earth. This Sound is acted upon and the Work is Sealed and Dispatched.

The second of these is *disengagement* from the particles of power by the group below the lighted temple; this group in formation disengages completely from the Work and henceforth is assisted in realigning energies within the formation to allow reintegration on the physical level and re-attuning to their lower vehicles.

The third of these is *closure* of the formation; a return to a steady state of beingness. It is essential that closure is completed efficiently and with time for balancing, each with the other, and for return of physical focus and being. To have undergone this journey with Us, to have served Him and mankind in this way, is to become a living lighted being, fully in control of his nature at that time, fully participative in an Ashramic effort and fully in tune with his soul's purpose in service to the One.

The more one serves, the more one receives, and so, in service to the plan, the disciple receives more acceleration in his life which can mean delineation in his auric field of possibilities for transmutative work. Thus, individual disciples approach the initiatory experience more readily when engaged in hierarchical group work than might otherwise be the case, leading to precipitation of karmic responsibility which may cause a minor, albeit sometimes decisive, disturbance of the lower vehicles. This will always pass and be the more beneficial if esoteric law is followed; we teach and nurture Our disciples in the ways of the journey of light.

The formative stages of the formation should provide for an *exclusion encirclement* of light around the participants. From Our perspective we use six encirclements to protect and focus certain energies which are given by Us and lifted from earth. The first of these is centered in the middle of the Twelve radiating outwards and blending with the second which encompasses in a band the participants.

The third of these, the *exclusion encirclement*, is around the outside of the formation, the fourth blends from that to the fifth and finally the sixth which is encompassing and focusing light in circuitous motion. Each of these encirclements is devised for protective purposes. Those that *Stand in the Light in waiting* should not pass the *exclusion encirclement* except when called to do so for purpose of the work.

Before the formation is enacted a period of protective encirclement should unfold as has been the case, successfully, heretofore. This energetic work combines with Ours to achieve the desired occult effects. The desired evolution of the process will necessitate no guidance from within the third encirclement. At this time, it is appropriate in preparatory Twelves to undertake this activity, however, I shall apprise my interpreter of timing. The future shall bring a trained organism, well trained in the art of this work, and it shall work in silence apart from certain Words of Power given by the North disciple indicating to all the nature and application required.

We shall have, then, three stages of Twelves development; the first preparatory which utilises the guidance of one who has been trained and is trusted by the ashram to safely fulfil this role, acting in the third encirclement.

The second is a group which has encompassed this activity by integrating the guidance within the Twelve and has progressed to initiating application by Words of Power, working consciously with the Ashram.

The third Twelve is one which consciously works with the Rays and is formed and completed at Our request with efficacy. This group has achieved a close collaboration, in full consciousness, with the Heart of the Ashram, in full silence with Words of Power received from Ashramic sources guiding the work. It is this last group who shall be engaged in participatory initiatory work of real significance. And now to talk of Rays, My friends, you have heard Me talk before of the Ray work of the Twelves and I would here bring to your conscious awareness again this concept of three types of Twelve. Dear brothers, We have worked with you on the Second Ray aspects of this outpouring with some Third Ray work and very little First Ray (but some nonetheless). At some future time, I shall be asking you to focus, from Approach stage, on a line of intent. This line shall be of the nature of one of the Rays (inclusive of its Sub-Ray structure) and certain advantages, esoterically, accrue for Us to have you poised. Facilitation is improved, flow heightened and application more the easier when all

stages of the bridge are conscious of the energy transference.

Brothers be not downhearted; your intent is enough
and will grow into appreciation and conscious cooperation
in due time. It is not necessary for all to achieve the same
consciousness to reap results; some will serve by Standing,
some by Application and some by fully Conscious Integration, all serve.

To those who *Stand in the Light in waiting*, a special
mention I shall give herewith, such a contribution is sorely
needed by Us and is, in itself, a part of the process and
gives indications to Us of service. This is not an idle
process but a Standing Forth of Light which is utilised by
the lighted beings, each bridge needs its supporting
structure!

The Brotherhood of the Star is especially active at this
time in the great vortexes which require a cleansing
process to invigorate the linkages so creating more
stability in the web; London, New York, Moscow, Tokyo,
Darjeeling, Geneva, Rio de Janeiro, Berlin, Brussels,
Adelaide and Beijing have set up a *relationship*, a *presence of
linkage*, which shall be utilised by Us for the purposes of
preparation of the Subtle Architecture for Christ's Return.
The Brotherhood of the Star is His Brotherhood and at its
center He Stands. Remember always, dear brothers, that
you are reflecting Ashramic energy, acting as *transmission
agents* both during the concentrated work of formation and
during your lives afterwards.

Take up then the Banner and let it Unfurl!

Take Our Call and let it Transmit!

Take Our Master's Love and let it Shine!

The Initiate, Ashram K.H., 1999

BURNING GROUND TWELVES

$\mathcal{T}$here is a basic assumption at the heart of every esotericist no matter what they believe and practice: that there is more to existence than can be perceived and known through the five senses. We are drawn to teachings that offer a coherent portrayal of a subtle reality. It's one thing to be drawn to esotericism, to study and absorb the knowledge, and another to put what you know into practice. Twelves continues to develop and refine its group practices and the most powerful ritual at the time of writing is Burning Ground Twelves.

When I re-joined, the BGT ritual was performed once a month, helping to build a weekly rhythm of group work which includes the Full and New Moon rituals and the TAM. Twelves national groups (based in Cuba, Mexico, USA, France, Italy, Slovenia and India) are self-organising and function autonomously while remaining true to the protocols. The Slovenian Twelves are especially dedicated, performing the Twelves protocol daily. All other Twelves followed the weekly rhythm.

When war broke out in Ukraine, the whole Twelves group responded to a strong sense of urgency, feeling the need to make the call for help, to form a bridge through which spiritual energies can descend to humanity. Burning Ground Twelves became weekly, with around three Twelves formed out of the general pool, with the national groups also participating.

Burning Ground Twelves, or BGT, has its roots in the Temple of Light. Steven originally came up with the name Burning Ground Protocol, which Vita then changed to the rather catchy sounding Burning Ground Twelves. Here is Vita's introduction to the protocol:

BURNING GROUND TWELVES

66 Humanity's evolution has been punctuated by moments of genius, spiritual awakenings and learning by trial and error. Step by step humanity has moved from survival mode to more complex modes of acting that involved the physical, astral, emotional, mental and buddhic levels of being. At each step we created 'good and bad' karma. At each incarnation we burned off some of that, often through difficult lessons on our paths. Adding to this there are collective pools of unresolved, outdated and dense matter impeding the influx of light.

Today, this part of the universe, our Earth and thus humanity is moving from the age of Pisces to the Age of Aquarius and such transitions require that old patterns be released. This is true on a personal as well as a collective level. The new energies require new vessels. Humanity therefore finds itself at this crossroad, a time that requires profound changes and the smashing up of the old is visible on all levels.

Evolution is about moving into better modes of being and of living. Through insights and progressive awakenings individuals transform themselves and step through gates of awareness by releasing old outmoded ways of being. This releasing is done through the 'fire of light' – the individual is now on the burning ground...

However, it is important to realise that transitions on such a cosmic scale are planetary and thus affect great swathes of outdated patterns and systems. This breaking up can be traumatic unless those involved move with the tide and into the new.

The Twelves experiment has been initiated with the aid of the Hierarchy, and more specifically, those initiates that are part of the Brotherhood of the Star. The Burning Ground Twelves use the geometrical formations, each made up of four (4) triangles, to create a vortex that uses the potency of Light, Love and Power to burn through those pools of unresolved matter, and through those 'cracks' let Light flood through to release such energy. This will allow for a more graceful transition.

— VITA DE WAAL

There is no better way to understand Burning Ground Twelves than to read a transcript of the ritual. Steven performs the role of focaliser. It should be noted that Steven's commentary is entirely unscripted.

BURNING GROUND TWELVES

Transcript March 7, 2022

BGT1

- T1 – T H, S H, P W
- T2 – J G, J R, M C
- T3 – M B, B K, W C
- T4 – M H, S A, T T

BGT2

- T1 – M S, C C, D H
- T2 – P K, T J, D S
- T3 – S O, R H, C L (B D filled in)
- T4 – K O, L M, D I

Supporters: C L, C K, G B, L. F T, S P, S R K Y, S A

STEVEN

WELCOME, as we come together for this sacred duty with love and humility for our world, let us remember as we walk this path to do so dispassionately, impersonally, without focusing on individuals, of who is right and who is wrong, we seek only to bring light and love and to be a conduit for our Hierarchy of Love.

AND AS THE world struggles to find itself, let us remember that as we move forward into 2025 and beyond, much muck is raised to the surface of humanity to be cleansed, transmuted and healed. Let us come together hand in hand, soul to soul.

LET US NOW VISUALISE A BOX, and in that box place all those things which are not needed at this time. All those concerns with our incarnation can be set aside for the sacred hour which we dedicate to our Hierarchy as Servants of Light.

So, together, let us walk the path of light and love and healing.

BELL

S O
Ceremony of Protection[1]

BELL

S H
The Great Invocation

BELL

STEVEN

So as we join together in our sacred task, let us visualise our place within the New Group of World Servers, focusing the light and love directed to our world from Shambala via our Spiritual Hierarchy. Breathe in that light through the crown chakra; let it permeate your being.

BELL

D S

Assembly of the Triangles

Let us begin to assemble the Triangles. T1, please step forward and create a Triangle of Light, Love and Power between you and visualise a golden triangle of living fire that burns not but ever heals, linking at your heart level and beginning to descend slowly to the earth.

Triangle Two please step forward; create a triangle one meter above T1, visualise your golden flaming Triangle beginning at your heart level and proceed towards the earth.

. . .

T3 STEP FORWARD, creating your Triangle one meter above T1 and T2; see and feel this triangle of golden healing fire linking your hearts and beginning to move down towards the earth itself, connecting an entire, empowered ?? by its energy until it reaches the others and welds with them.

T4 STEP FORWARD, creating your Triangle one meter above T1, T2 and T3. See and feel this triangle of living fire linking your hearts and beginning getting to move down to the earth as well until it reaches the others and welds with them, creating this radiant, golden-flaming 12-Star of light and love and power.

BELL

STEVEN

ABOVE US AND through us the vortex begins to form, linking Shambalic energies through the layers of infinity. And we remember our coworkers scattered throughout infinity, working with the one Light that we all serve.

BELL

D I
The Disciples Invocation

BELL

STEVEN

AND ABOVE THE TWELVE FORMATION, a point of light forms and glows and swells as the vortex of love descends through our formations as a conduit of love, power and healing. And before us, our world spinning as it does within our universe, shrouded in greyness, interspersed with the points of Light crying for assistance to transmute and heal the past; to visualise the present and prepare for the future. And as the great Beings of Light approach us, let us welcome them, and the Great Devas attend us. We, a point of Light within the ring-pass-not of the New Group of World Servers, do dedicate our service activity to the Lord of Love, whose undoubted presence is with us always.

A SPIRAL of Light descends and passes out through the 12 points of our formations and our supporters stand and assist with open hearts and loving minds. Let us communicate now with those many beings that surround us as we understand that we here incarnate beings on the endpoint in a great flow of energy from far off places and we here, now, accept that loving energy through our formations that we might focus in service of our co workers.

. . .

LET us invoke the light and love with the Great Devas and we become the chalice of love.

The Devic Prayer

GREAT DEVIC LORD hear our prayer. We invoke thy light as it is written, the time of need has come, come forth o Mighty One, bring forth thy fiery wisdom. Join with the Master alike of angels and men. Bring forth the chalice anew. Come forth O Mighty One, enjoin with us on Earth. Pour forth the waters of joy, pour forth the waters of peace, pour forth the waters of healing. Come forth, O Mighty One. We, the children of Earth, invoke O protector and divine Power. Smite the unclean and raise the transmuted ones, we invoke thee now in thy presence and in all thy glory, come forth o Mighty One.

AND SO WE pray to thee, come. And so we invoke thee, come. And so we serve thee, come. Come with thy hordes of light, we implore thee in the name of the One Initiator. Hear our call. The time is here, the testing has begun. We lose our fear and embrace thy love eternal. Alight our our hearts with love.

COME FORTH NOW, be amongst us and within us, we who seek to serve, pour forth thy light upon our earth. O Lord of Life, come forth. OM OM OM

. . .

So LET us visualise our beautiful planet, and we see about it a dark cloud of ancient darkness. And through our formations, a point of fire descends, and descending thus, passes through the vortex and through us. And let us visualise this fire of light and love penetrating the dark cloud of ancient darkness. We beseech the Hierarchy of Light, use us now as thy instrument of peace upon this Burning Ground. Visualise the fire entering this ancient dark thought-form and penetrating thus dissolving and healing as it burns and transmutes this dark web which invades our earth. Let us free those souls who play with it thus, burning away their connection where love should be.

LET us now tarry awhile as the Master approaches.

I SEEK the way I yearn to know visions I see and fleeting deep impressions behind the portal on the other side lies that which I call home, for the circle has been well-nigh trod and the end approaches the beginning. I seek the way, all ways my feet have trod. The way of fire calls me with fierce appeal. Naught in me seeks the way of peace, naught in me yearns for earth. Let the fire rage, let the flames devour, let all the dross be burned, and let me enter through that gate and tread the way of fire. OM OM OM

MASTER, use our formations for Light, accept our fiery triangles into thy chalice. We invoke thee from the depths of our Souls, heal our earth this day. And the fire burns and transmutes and separates into many pieces. As we visualise the Burning Ground of love slowly, we transform the thought-form into Light, and we are conscious cooperators with Hierarchy. Now let us pour forth the waters of healing, healing of souls, and we invoke the angels of healing to accept into their loving embrace those souls transitioning at this time. And we invoke peace for our earth, for every being therein, peace and love and healing.

GREAT HIERARCHY OF LIGHT, use our formations as instruments of thy healing. Let the waters of Aquarius pour forth, not just this day but forever, and may our leadership be touched by compassion and love, and may thy hand touch the hearts of all. The purpose of my soul must show itself through burning, that which obstructs and hinders must disappear before the power of God. That power am I.

I, therefore, tread the way unto the Burning Ground; there, hindrances disappear. My will is one with the Great Will of God. That will is mine today upon the planes of earth. It leads to service and my masters group. I, therefore, tread the way of service after the Festival of Burning. I dedicate myself to the purpose of the Plan, I have no purpose but the Will of God. I seek no other way but the way of divine fulfilment. I lose myself within the group which seeks the furtherance of the Plan.

BECOME ONE WITH OUR PURPOSE, dear friends, as we walk the way with the World Teacher, and in whose service we aspire to be a lighted-way for others, and the waters pour forth from the vessel of Aquarius bringing succour to the world of human-kind. And when we leave this place, let us take our ashramic duty and love in our daily lives and in our Triangles of Fire lest we forget our purpose on earth is to be the representation of the externalisation of our

Hierarchy. These are not idle words, these are a living Fire, let it become thus.

I WILL NOW RECITE the World Teacher invocation. Join with me, deep within your hearts and souls as we touch the hem of the Lord of Light and we bring forth the Power and the Light and the Love that stretches forth from Shambala through our beloved Hierarchy and the New Group of World Servers to the incarnate world. The Hierarchy are very close to us and hear our soul-yearning, and in humbleness I throw my soul into the fire of service, accept my humble offering, Lord of Light.

The World Teacher Invocation

GREAT LORD OF LIGHT, hear our prayer. We before thee, come to offer service, we before thee come to offer supplication, we before thee, offer all that we are. We invoke thee and thy hosts of Light. We beseech thee to hear our call, we offer thee our lines of intent. From out of the world of Mankind doth come the call; come aid us in our hour of need, come lead us to thy Holy Fire, come heal our broken world. As it has been written, so shall it be. Great Lord, command our souls in thy Army of Light, we place before thee our all. We, thy vanguard, have eyes half shut. Awaken us, wherever we may be, let us sleep no more. Let light enter and darkness be gone. Great Teacher, hear our supplication, come again into our hearts that we may know thy wonder. We invoke thee, in all thy power and love. Lord of Compassion, pour upon us the healing balm that we may be whole once more. Great Lord, we touch the hem of thy garment that we may be at one with thy divine purpose. Let us this day and forevermore. Lord, let us become a channel for thy love, let us smite the darkness and let in thy glory. Great Lord of Light, hear our prayer. Where once we were lost, now we are found. Great Lord, we invoke thee.

BELL

L M
The Great Invocation

BELL

D S
Dissolution of the Triangles

BEFORE THE DISSOLUTION of the Twelve-Star, let us regard it for a moment with awe and gratitude, this fiery assemblage of healing Triangles.

AND NOW, beginning with T4, attend to your Triangle. Allow it to detach and rise above the others. Release it and watch as it dissolves and disappears.

• • •

T3, please attend to your Triangle. Separate and lift it from the others, those that remain. Witness its dissolution as it slowly disappears.

T2, now follow suit in attending to your Triangle; gently detaching and lifting and allow it to fade from view.

AND FINALLY, T1 upon which the Twelve was built, allow your Triangle to rise and dissolve and recede.

AND AS WE in the Twelve step back, we feel the remaining energies receding and disburse to wherever they are needed. We give thanks to all angels, devas, souls, supporters who guided, witnessed and protected this work. We give gratitude to hear and answer the call; the call to serve. Blessed be, Amen.

BELL

K O
Closing Prayer

LET us give thanks for the work we have done together today. We are grateful to all the Twelves and all the workers throughout the world for the work they are doing. We are grateful to be part of what we are doing together, with the same purpose. We are grateful to the devas, we are grateful to the enlargement of the Plan, we are grateful to the Mahachohan, the Manu, Bhagavan Krishna, to the great Architect of the Universe. We are grateful to each and every living being who is constantly working toward the development of humanity. We are always grateful for the past, present and future New Group of World Servers. We are always grateful to be a part of the nations who have laid their life, who have sacrificed their lives, for the sake of the welfare of humanity. Let us show our gratitude and love to all the living beings on this planet. OM OM OM

BELL

STEVEN
The Great Invocation

BELL

S A
The Great Invocation in his native language.

STEVEN

AT YOUR FEET there is a box, take from it what you will.
Blessings to each one of you and may peace come to our
earth. Thank you, namaste.

* * *

IT IS clear from this transcript that Twelves work is not for
the faint-hearted. As Vita states:

> You must be available uninterrupted, undis-
> turbed, and focused (no doorbells, phones,
> cats, or dogs). You will need silence, a glass of
> pure water and a mute button on everything.
> [And] It is essential that none of us impart any
> of our own prejudice into this process. You
> may have personal opinions regarding poli-
> tics, religious or cultural issues – there is no
> place for them in occult work. If this is a chal-
> lenge for you, just ask, 'can I set these aside for
> now while I work?' If you feel you cannot
> undertake this impartially and cannot set
> aside your personality preferences, then this
> work is not for you. It can cause some disrup-
> tion to you in your present incarnation.

---

1. See appendix

THE COLLECTIVE
EXPERIENCE OF TWELVES

I asked Twelves participants to write about their impression of the group as a whole and its purpose, and to relate any experiences during the rituals that they may have had. As is evident in a previous chapter, although there are commonalities, everyone approaches Twelves from their own highly individual background and experience. All are motivated to affect positive change in the world drawing on the subtle planes in a highly structured magical process. This time, I have presented these contributions without any commentary, instead allowing the reader to become fully immersed in the testimony. Here's what they said:

Vita

My work in Twelves has been to present the teachings in a more universal language while at the same time reminding all that this is not DK-informed work – albeit it is Ashram related and within that lineage, that family, a different branch of the same tree – and to bring to the fore the concept that these traditions evolve in response to the needs of the time. I don't glamourise the work and trust that those who need to come will come. Our work is also to make sure that they can find us, hence my work on the website.

Others hear bells, see things, and even get visits. I have none of these but seem to know what I need to do. Yes, of course I would love to get tangible signs but to execute and bring into reality is my 'reward' – to somehow know what next and what needs doing and then see the growth and evolution of Twelves. To be seamless with Steven but in such a different manner.

DI

THE GROUP IS a community of the members who are scattered all over the world, yet able to connect and perform this service, so the Oneness is real, the connection is real, and the energies are real. I think we are making a definite contribution to humanity and our planet, thus aiding in the transformation and hopefully planetary initiation at some point. Also, the special formation of 12 members is as powerful as perhaps several hundred or thousands of people meditating in a group without this structure.

A great teacher, Grandmaster Choa Kok Sui, the founder of the modern Pranic Healing and the Arhatic Yoga, said that if seven people meditate together that equals hundred people meditating by themselves in terms of energy generated or transformed from the Divine sources and the Hierarchy.

Can you imagine what a special twelve-star formation can do?

The Twelves meditations are very special and quite an intense experience. There is a lovely spirit of community, serving together, and also growing spiritually as a group. Having a community of international friends with the similar spiritual interests is a true blessing and a priceless experience.

The energies of Full Moon and New Moon are generally loving and ray 2, leaving you filled with love and bliss.

The first BGT I did, I felt this crystal, clear energy, very, very refined, yet very strong, streaming through my body, and when my body started to overheat, the stream stopped. As if the Beings guiding it knew how much the incarnate bodies can take, and they stopped. The energies of the BGT are quite different than those of NM of FM, there is a definite power felt, although lately I feel the Presence of the World Teacher, more intensely every time we perform the BGT meditation.

The visualisations during the meditations are very vivid. I particularly remember the Diamond of the World Teacher swirling around so fast and with so much energy that, as if it was approaching me, I felt the urge to move my head away.

I also feel very strong presence of the World Teacher, both in TAM (The Ashramic Meditation) and the BGT (Burning Ground Twelve). Whenever we have TAM, once we enter the most inner circle of the Ashram, I feel that our group has an audience with the World Teacher, and for days after I feel this indescribable joy, lightness, very gentle sense of humour, Love in my heart and it is radiating outwards. I have noticed my family members, my pet doggie, people around me, are reacting in a more loving, gentle manner.

. . .

CS

I SINCERELY BELIEVE that Twelves work is very powerful in transforming the collective consciousness of humanity. I feel like the triangles work amplifies the energies of the Great Invocation and the Twelves work amplifies the triangles work even more.

Unfortunately, because of other responsibilities, I cannot always join the other activities done during the weekdays such as the Burning Ground Meditation. From what I have seen and experienced in participating within these occult meditations, these energies seem to evoke similar energies to those of the occult meditations given by Master DK. I have not experienced physical Twelves but from what I read in the book the *Esoteric Apprentice*, the occult meditations appear to follow the universal laws or principles of ceremonial Magick. The only difference is that the Twelves work aims for the betterment of all humanity.

I believe the Twelves work is an expansion and continuation of the esoteric teachings given by Master DK to Alice Bailey. The principles and objectives of the work follow the same principles as those given to the three great teachers: Helena Blavatsky, Alice Bailey, and Helena Roerich.

I do not consider myself sensitive to subtle energies. Even during the days when I was studying Wicca and Shamanism, I considered myself more adept at projecting energy than in receiving them. However, on several occasions during the Twelves work, I sometimes feel the energy response from the Deva in the portal. I felt its energy responding to the group's collective invocation. I believe that these meditations truly help in expanding the collective consciousness of humanity. It is a definite stepping stone to help in Materialising the Divine Plan on Earth.

KO

AFTER JOINING TWELVES, I found many of my Theosophy friends in the group. I have gone through the website and found the website very helpful and understood that the group associated with this site have a very good plans to serve humanity. The Meditations are of high quality, and I felt a tremendous flow of energy many times from the POINT OF LOVE. As I am very much into spiritual work these meditations helped me to find ways to travel towards LIGHT full of ENERGY and WISDOM. I submit myself to the Initiatee with pure awareness during these meditations and put my efforts to vacate myself thus the INITIATEE can find me and my vehicles a good transmitter of energies.

RH

TWELVES IS about making an antahkarana or bridge of Light for the reappearance of the Christ as per The Great Invocation dictated by Master D.K. to Alice Bailey, and to work so that in the next conclave of the Spiritual Hierarchy in 2025 the best decisions for the planet and humanity are made.

Through global meditation, aided by invocations and visualisations of a vortex of Light from which the Light, love and power of great beings who know and serve God's plan on earth descend, we pave the way for the fulfilment of the plan of love and Light and close the door where there is evil.

Our commitment as world servers is first to align our life with the purpose that the Masters know and serve and second to work for the dissemination of this purpose.

The group of twelves that we have formed with the participation of our colleagues in Mexico, Puerto Rico and Cuba, is due to the integration that we have had for years working under the coordination of Carmen Santiago, a task that was easy to understand because we had already worked before as a group for the formation of the connection with Shambhala and the reappearance of the Christ.

All this work has enriched my life and that of our family, as it has caused the seeds of light sown in our hearts due to teaching and service to leaven a peace and stability that keeps us in balance despite external imbalances. We are very fortunate and we thank the Spiritual Hierarchy for allowing us to be part of this beautiful planetary healing service and to be able to do our bit for the transformation of our own lives and that of this planet.

So we work on forgetting ourselves, harmlessness and the correct word, always guided by internal wisdom that like a torch of light points out the path of our service on this beautiful planet.

KTMW

As an astrologer and a student of ancient wisdom I know that group work is the future. Telepathic group work especially. I also know that 2025 is an important year. I feel that this is a part of what we have been training for all along, and that we need to take action. Now!

Also, group work is a continuation of the work

Bailey/DK started. I had an inner calling and clarity knowing that this is right! When I have those types of dreams it's like I don't really have a choice. It's just an inner impulse of something I just have to do. I feel in many ways that Twelves is that advanced group I have been waiting for, to work with. Where we all have an inner fire that burns for God's plan on earth. That we are willing to be of service to humanity, to be humble, to be loving and wise. To take responsibility.

Regarding our inner impulses in these special difficult times, we have the opportunity to take a collective initiation as humanity. Love is service. Service is love. I trust this group. It feels right and pure.

There is no time to waste. I am happy to see that the group is growing and the impulse is alive and strong.

I also genuinely feel that all my life, my search, my studies and my contribution has led up to these specific times in humanity and that I am grateful to be a part of an impulse, a group and an egregore that has the focus to help humanity forward.

I have meditated for many years and been a part of several triangles before. My experience of Twelves meditations (New Moon, Full Moon, Burning Ground) is that these are advanced and that the souls that meet in these meditation rooms know what they are doing. There is a pureness to it and a higher purpose. We leave our personal stuff outside to enter the room of ritual on the meditation plane to work as a soul tribe of love and wisdom.

JGGA

BEING part the group meditation of the Twelve has a feeling of oneness and a bigger service That comes with a lot of energetic downpour and bliss.

The group as whole is loving and welcoming family and light beings with similar purpose and goal to be of service as channels and anchors of light.

JGG

I'M NOT a person who regularly hears and sees things, but I am energetically sensitive. My very first Twelve, I was practically swept off my feet by the energy generated by Twelve Disciples joined in intention, and by the vortex that descends during the meditation. I have no doubt of the power and efficacy of our endeavours, and I am humbled and grateful that I am able to join with so many others of Goodwill in being a part of it. I am aware that I am being 'used' at all times as a channel, a transformer, a conduit. As we said at the end of our rituals in Gaia's Circle, 'The Circle is Open but Unbroken'. The Twelve is open but remains. We are generating at all times. Conscious and real time connection multiplies the power but it is there, waiting to be reenergised. I try to stay in that awareness, but, being human, I slip up. I see that striving and that humanness in all in the Twelves Group. That makes me love the group and the people in it all the more. We come from different backgrounds, experiences, cultures, countries, politics, etc. We are able to set aside differences, even value and celebrate them in a way that is inspiring and is the goal for all Humanity. Together we enter sacred space and join in common purpose, the manifesting of the truths set forth by The Great Invocation:

May Light Descend on Earth
May Christ Return to Earth
May Purpose Guide the Little Wills of Men

May the Door Where Evil Dwells Be Sealed
Let Light, Love and Power Restore the Plan on Earth.

SEO

THERE ARE many different ways that people connect with the world of meaning, that which we discern in the process of meditation. My connection is through sensing, feeling and knowing.

The Full Moon meditations, when practiced ardently, often later (over the course of days or sometimes weeks) bring insights that illuminate blockages that need to be addressed, both personal and in service to others.

New Moon meditations result in a strengthened feeling of brotherhood and strengthened group service.

Burning Ground meditations are something quite different. The crescendo of approach is the ardent path to the top of the mountain. It is palpable, sometimes arduous, and always filled with anticipation. Once at the top, the Burning Ground meditation itself is sometimes uncomfortable, much like how a bright, bright light may be uncomfortable. The return back down is a feeling of shedding, and the discomfort here is often from newly exposed areas, somewhat likened to the itch of healing. Burning dross is not easy, is sometimes uncomfortable (or even painful), but is always satisfying. The experience of the Burning Ground meditation itself is one of purification and release.

The Ashram Meditations bring me closer to a place of knowing, of purpose. The first experiences were like touching the hem of the garment of the Ashram. With time, it grew into beingness of a thread in the weave of the garment.

182 | SPIRITUAL CHANGEMAKERS

There are many groups composed of individuals who work toward a common objective. It is rare to find a group in which individuals fuse into group service. It is also rare to find 'service' in an elemental form—love light and power directed unimpeded and without the lens of interpretation or intention.

LM

I THINK that the Twelves group is well organised, and in the group, there are really many professionals and researchers with a lot of knowledge and wisdom. I am really happy to be part of it. I also feel a lot of love, loving kindness and respect. I feel at home. I think that the purpose of the group is really important in this period of time and it is vital to contribute to raise the frequency of the earth.

RB

MY MEDITATIONS ARE NOT AT ALL spectacular. I always have a hard time visualising. Instead, I am able to perceive my higher chakras with ease. During my first Twelve meditation on the January 2019 full moon, the perception of the chakras was spectacular. I was in India and the exact time of the full moon coincided with a flight I was taking from Chennai to Delhi. I did the meditation on the plane. The Heart chakra and the Third Eye were very active and I felt a pulsating movement between these two chakras and then between the Heart chakra and the Crown chakra. I had never experienced such intensity before, except the previous year in a South Indian temple dedicated to Lord Dattatreya, to whom I am very devoted and who represents the Trinity.

My Geminian nature makes me jump from one spiritual tradition to another, from one group to another, from one practice to another. With Twelves I feel very involved. Since the beginning of the present phase, I have not stopped participating and my feeling is that I will never stop. The group is compact, very active and very conscious.

EB

A LIVED EXPERIENCE (hasn't that always been my wish?) is offered in Twelves and moreover at the service of the Hierarchy. My Rosicrucian studies already spoke to us of the invisible Masters and now I have the opportunity to serve them, even very modestly of course.

I have been in Twelves for a short time, and I know that the experimentation of the group will be useful because it was proposed by the Initiate of the Ashram of Master KH, set up and relayed to allow men to express their desire of justice and peace.

May this testimony be of service to the readers, a strong motivation filled with convictions leads to all paths. Taking the right path is the challenge!

CC

WHEN I FIRST JOINED THE Twelves, I knew it was the group for me as it engendered a feeling of 'coming home'. All the meditation work was familiar and slotted effortlessly into my daily life. The group development was on the whole slow and steady, but sometimes experienced sudden growth spurts as new members brought particular skills with them that were utilised by the group to aid its expansion. Members have come and gone but the core group of dedicated workers has increased and their commitment has grown. The energy that the group now generates and the light it is beginning to emit is discernible and its work is moving forward dynamically and its magnetic centre has started to attract more and more people into its ranks.

JR

BEING TRAINED in visualising during meditation has been a real bonus, although of late it is much more energetic, for example seeing only light effects and patterns rather than anything resembling life on earth.

LFT

IN NEW MOON'S meditation on January 2, 2022, I had the chance to participate in a support role, although my visualisation focused on being around the circles of twelves, the image in my mind directed me to see myself in the middle of all the circles formed on that day, together with other members I didn't know, and focusing in strengthening the energy of all those who were in the twelve star formations. But also, around everyone, there were some other support members and many souls and beings without a body who had decided to actively participate in the process, supporting and creating a wall of light.

As the vortexes of light were formed within the groups of twelves, I was able to see an ascended being of Light in the center of one of them and he communicated to me that this energetic force allowed him to manifest more fully on the Earthly planes, and that the twelve groups of twelves were needed for the manifestation of twelve ascended masters who were ready to perform another twelve pointed star formation themselves. He used the phrase '*As above, so below*', to manifest on the physical plane a much more powerful level of energy vibration passing through the different limiting layers of density.

Next full moon meditation was when the twelve groups of twelves were finally formed.

My impression of the group, in the short time that I have been a participant is that kindness and cooperation reign, something that I have discovered is usually rare in other groups of spiritual or esoteric knowledge and teachings, where criticism and competition seems evident; in addition to noticing that the purpose of the group involves people who show a lot of dedication and desire for knowledge, which empowers everybody.

PW

The Twelves meditation utilises group and ashramic alignment.

I NOW PARTICIPATE in a rhythmic cycle of Full Moon and New Moon Twelves work, interspersed with live Burning Ground meditations. As an intelligent response to need and opportunity, I believe that the work of Twelves is a useful part of the plan to prepare the way for the Christ and the externalization of the Spiritual Hierarchy.

The Twelves meditation provides the group structure required to energise the pre-existing network of Triangles, and for the hard-line work of dissolving thought-forms in humanity's collective astral body. The meditation begins with group alignment and permits four groups of Triangles to each invoke the energy of the three Rays, which can be understood as evoking a response from extra-planetary forces in the form of a vortex of Light, Love and Power, which descends through Shambala and our Spiritual Hierarchy and into the Minds, Hearts and the individual Will centres in mankind. This, in turn, flows outward from the NGWS and into general humanity as purpose, good-will and intelligent activity.

The Twelves meditation is structured upon true occult
principles

ESOTERIC TRADITION ASSURES us that 'energy follows thought' and the Christ Jesus confirmed that His presence would be found wherever disciples gathered in groups of two or three in His name.* In the books of the Law of One,** RA alluded that the power of ceremonial group devotion, prayer and meditation is magnified according to the number and quality of the practitioners and the geometric form of their resultant structure.

Armed with these types of assurances, practitioners from all Paths can rest assured that the unique meditative form utilised by the Twelves is calculated to operate in accordance with cosmic and systemic laws as taught across many religions. I believe that the Twelves service meditations are a wise use of our free-will as disciples, and are an effective tool help anchor the Christ-Consciousness upon the planet.

SH

From the genuine warm welcome I received from the members, and the very first Twelve I participated in, I felt I had come home. The more I participated, the more I wanted to do; this was where I was meant to be and serve. Each meditation is done in service, ever increasing in power, and I am always humbled and honoured to serve with this amazing group of souls from all corners of the world.

TS

After 18 months of practicing Twelves, I can wholeheartedly say that what Steven wrote in *Esoteric Apprentice*, that 'anyone that ever takes part in a Twelve is deeply affected by it on many levels. It IS a work and service that should not be underestimated', is very real and true for me. I am really grateful to him, that he picked up the work where it got stuck in the 90s.

However, what is most important, is loving assistance and service that participants are offering to the betterment of the world's situation through the Twelves work which increases the certainty for the Externalisation of the Hierarchy in 2025.

. . .

TH

MY IMPRESSION OF TWELVES' purpose as a whole is to be an inlet for Divine and Cosmic-Spiritual Shamballic and Hierarchically transmitted Light-Love-Power energies for world transformation, world enlightenment, world healing, world inspiration, world unity/interconnectedness and world change in these times of special planetary need and crisis in the transiting process from the Age of Pisces to Aquarius.

The Twelves Project serves as a New Hierarchical Ashramic Occult Planetary Antahkaranic Bridge to strengthen, stabilise and secure the Distribution of Aquarian Cosmic-Stellar and Solar-(Uranus-Jupiter), Shamballa and Hierarchical Energies to the Earthly form-planes of Human Civilisation helping the Planetary Transformation and Initiation process towards becoming a Holy Planet.

The Twelves Meditations I understand and experience are as 'A new form of Group-Mandala Ritualistic Meditations' and an expansion, combination and amplification of the hitherto given Triangles-exercises (Great Invocation Group-Prayer Practice) and the suggested Full Moon and New Moon exercises and Services suggested by the Spiritual Hierarchy.

I have various experiences from time to time but some of the most consistent is that this particular energy work seems to be easier and more powerful in Twelve Group Formation and via the daily Triangles exercises and via the Twelves Heart-Chakra Group, such as the Flower-Mandala formation on the Full Moons and New Moons, and on the Burning Ground world-transformational and healing meditations carried out by the Meditators together.

But also the group vortex experiences are very powerful, involving Archangelic and The Unified Hierarchical Masterfield experiences (I experience the Hierarchy as A Planetary Heart-Center Twelve of Masters with Christ as Centerpoint and an overshadowing supportive Triangle of Buddha, Spirit of Peace, and Avatar of Synthesis.

PATRICK CHOUINARD

WE ARE TOLD by DK that the soul is self-consciousness (not in the egoistic sense), group conscious (inclusive), and God-conscious (conscious that it is part of and subordinate to a greater Being or whole).

Group-consciousness is not uniformity or conformity of consciousness, or a hive-like 'group-think' phenomenon. It is the individual consciousness (for we always remain individuals no matter what spiritual stage we are in) freely uniting with other individuals - an inclusive consciousness - that while being self-conscious or aware is not self-absorbed but directed outwards in love toward others (like a Sun which radiates).

This involves giving our best to the group as individuals – in service to the group. I have not always done so.

I learned that our soul is part of a Universal Soul, like a cell in our body (all spiritual cells or souls being vibrationally interconnected) and the physical plane is the body of a cosmic Being (just as our bodies are vehicles for the soul).

Collectively humanity is a group, though few see or feel themselves as members of this great family. The soul does. Included is the realisation that we cannot be truly free and happy individually until we are all free and happy, because we are all interconnected and interdependent.

No man is an island unto himself, they say. We either help or hinder the collective spiritual progress through every thought and action, and when we harm others, we are also hurting ourselves. And hurting ourselves lovelessly harms humanity.

This is something to take to heart where our Twelves' work is concerned. This is basic esotericism but it has taken me many years to really live with that awareness, to take that to heart (such is the selfishness of human nature, of the ego). I still remind myself. I know more than I can do.

The role of the white magician is to stimulate the light in others and others and to help in the manifestation of that Plan – to become an agent or servant of the Forces of Light – light not only symbolically but literally the spiritual light or energies of enlightenment (wisdom) and of love (seen as a force, reminiscent of Star Wars). White magic is the magic of love, the most powerful force of all (when we have the power to love all lesser powers or forces are ours to command).

The theosophical or occult energy concept was new to me, but instantly made sense. There was much talk of energy in the Twelves group and soon these energies became part of my direct experience.

I was really struck by this idea that impacting the etheric body of the planet – of humanity – with light and love, would also impact humanity in time. Spiritual energies have been blocked or impeded in the flow of energies from higher levels to the dense physical. A dense heavy cloud of negative energy surrounds humanity and our planet (psychic pollution) impeding the circulation of love and light (talked about much in the Agni Yoga books). Through Twelves we pierce this barrier and invoke light and love, and then become a group conduit for those energies to circulate within the planetary etheric grid, raising its vibration (and where the light goes the forces of evil must fade away). Their stronghold on the physical plane will be broken.

Sometimes I have doubted the real usefulness of this type of work. Am I really helping the world? However, I have learned from my reading and experience that meditation and service is a way to contact the soul – to synchronise with it so to speak –and that we can be of real service especially through group meditation, which amplifies the energy (furthermore certain higher energies require a group as a conduit, being too powerful for individuals to contain and transmit).

I have no doubt the Twelves ritual establishes that funnel DK talks about (both sound and colour are used extensively in the Twelves ritual). I completely trust that this is the esoteric service I am called to do at this time of world crisis and spiritual opportunity (preceding 2025).

I really feel the difference between my personal meditations and the group meditations. In The Esoteric Apprentice Steven talks about how powerfully members of Twelves felt the energy. Truly it is like being overshadowed, a heightening, and that for me is the best psychic experience I could ask for. I feel that too in our distant Twelves work, though I am sure it will be more powerful when we do our Twelves work in person.

Through Twelves we are helping to open the channel between the kingdom of souls and the human kingdom. We are helping to link them (through the funnel we create in our Twelves a kind of group antahkarana is formed) and so facilitating the establishment of the kingdom of God on Earth – the externalisation of the Hierarchy.

EXPERIENCES OF ONE
TWELVES ASHRAM
MEDITATION

DI

It was a wonderful meditation of very powerful loving, soothing energies. I was unable to type anything last night, I was blissed out. Thank you Steven and all the participants!

Murray

It was the most powerful TAM I have ever experienced; powerful in the way of deeply loving and soothing energies. It felt as if I and the whole group were entering a new phase of interconnection and deepest regard for each other.

Vita

I would like to add that in the last phase of our visit I sensed that each of us was taken 'by hand' by a lighted being who accompanied / guided us. To me this new phase of interconnection Murray mentions also regards our conscious cooperation with deeply loving beings from other evolutions. My deepest gratitude to all, and to Steven

CC

Totally agree. This TAM was a really profound experience which has really affected me deeply on a consciousness level. The group cohesion was beautiful not just earthly participants but the spiritual ones as well.

A CONCLUSION

$\mathcal{T}$welves can easily be dismissed by sceptics as a post-millennium cult holding some crazy attachment to a belief in the reappearance of the World Teacher. All spiritual practice is easily dismissed in the same way. Even if a sceptical position is adopted, there is something much deeper of value in Twelves. And that, put simply, concerns the group work itself. It's esoteric, both in the sense that metaphysical ideas sit at its foundation, and in its rituals of invocation, and also spiritual in the sense that higher beings and light itself are at the heart of the group. Above all, Twelves embodies esoteric group work, that is, groups of twelve coming together remotely, often in real time, to conduct a group meditation that cannot be effective without every participant involved. Even if you strip away all notions of the spiritual hierarchy and the significance of the year 2025, even if you don't believe either holds any truth, you are still left with an important example of white magic performed at its highest level; esoteric practice as both concept and service. Above all, participants in Twelves are responding to a felt sense of urgency. As Patrick Chouinard notes:

> The great push of the hierarchy (1965-2025) is not over, the tide is still with us and we can make a real impact through Twelves and in our daily lives. We are told that at this time every word spoken or written by a disciple is potent (more so in group formation).

> DK says disciples have more impact – for good or ill – than they realize (notwithstanding that some overestimate their status, importance and influence) and this high cycle of energy inflow (1965-2025) amplifies our potential impact even more.

ESOTERIC GROUP WORK of this nature is distinct from personality-based groups, including families, teams, workplace colleagues and committees. Personalities always impact the group dynamic and it is no different in a soul group, except that it's handled very differently. Performing daily and weekly occult rituals binds participants in ways that are subtle. There's an understanding that the group is connected on the inner planes to the larger group of souls, including Masters, angels and devas. And this deeper awareness creates changes in the way group members interact with one another. There's a tendency to think, ponder, assess. There's a keenness to speak and act from a position of loving service. Twelves continues to attract those with mystical and esoteric dispositions from around the globe. Twelves offers hope, just as all Theosophy offers hope of a better world.

I think Twelves is revolutionary. Twelves seeks human

and planetary betterment in a special way. Twelves is engaged in pure esoteric work following the Ageless Wisdom tradition, firmly on the side of the will to good and the will to love. Twelves is unique, highly specialised and a privilege to be a part of.

TWELVES CEREMONY OF PROTECTION

From the Twelve Points of the Star Let the Fire Burn

Let the Four Archangels Respond and see to Their Task

Let Them deliver unto the Sons of Men their destiny

From that Mighty Mountain let the One Return and Let the Plan Work Out

Let the Solar Pitris respond to the Initiator's Call

Let the Twelve points merge into One

From that One Let the Fire Burn Upon its Course

So, I petition Thee oh Archangel of the North

So, I petition Thee oh Archangel of the South

So, I petition Thee oh Archangel of the East

So, I petition Thee oh Archangel of the West

Let the One Initiator hear His disciples' Call

Bring Me your Rod of Iron

Bring Me your Solace Deep

Bring Me your Mighty Fire

Let the Workers respond to my Call

Let them go Upon Their Course at my Direction

I have laid bare my All and have set aside my chattels

I am ready for the Work.

And so, an unbroken circle is placed about us

We seek the Protection of our Ashram

And in the Name of The World Teacher we Invoke the Blessing and Protection

of the Overlighting Deva and the Lords of Love

OM OM OM

The City Invocation

Let the City of London, the City of New York and the City of Moscow

Be Aflame with the Light of Shamballa

Let the Outer Dross be Burnt Away

Let those therein Become One with the Divine Purpose

and May We Each do our Part

OM OM OM

Let the Builders Form and Fall away

Let the Note be Struck

Let those therein Reveal Their True natures

OM OM OM

Let the Will be Invoked

Let the Fire Burn

Let the Heart Chakra Respond

So, Let it Be

OM OM OM

ACKNOWLEDGMENTS

This book would not exist without the Twelves group and all who have shown support for the project. My heartfelt gratitude to all who have contributed to its creation. Warm thanks especially to Vita de Waal who willingly provided me with detailed testimony and got the ball rolling. I'm in awe of her focus, dedication and commitment. My deep thanks to Steven Chernikeeff who has been involved in this book project since its inception. And to all the mystics and occultists out there who strive to pour light and love into this world of ours, thank you!

* * *

Isobel Blackthorn holds a PhD for her ground breaking study of the texts of Theosophist Alice Bailey. She is the author of *Alice a. Bailey: Life and Legacy* and *The Unlikely Occultist: a biographical novel of Alice A. Bailey.* Isobel is also an award-winning novelist.

Made in United States
North Haven, CT
09 August 2022